ROLL AWAY YOUR STONE

BOOKS BY DUTCH SHEETS

FROM BETHANY HOUSE PUBLISHERS

Authority in Prayer
Roll Away Your Stone

ROLL AWAY YOUR STONE

LIVING IN THE POWER OF THE RISEN CHRIST

DUTCH SHEETS

BESTSELLING AUTHOR OF *Intercessory Prayer*

BETHANYHOUSE
MINNEAPOLIS, MINNESOTA

Roll Away Your Stone
Copyright © 2007
Dutch Sheets

Manuscript prepared by Marcus Yoars

Cover design by Lookout Design, Inc.
Cover photo by Gaylon Wampler

Published by Bethany House Publishers
11400 Hampshire Avenue South
Bloomington, Minnesota 55438

Bethany House Publishers is a division of
Baker Publishing Group, Grand Rapids, Michigan.

Printed in the United States of America

Hardcover: ISBN-13: 978-0-7642-0173-8   ISBN-10: 0-7642-0173-5
Audio CD: ISBN-13: 978-0-7642-0368-8   ISBN-10: 0-7642-0368-1

Library of Congress Cataloging-in-Publication Data

Sheets, Dutch.
    Roll away your stone : living in the power of the risen Christ / Dutch Sheets.   p.   cm.
    Summary: "The author reveals life-changing biblical truths about who we are in Christ and how to become the person God made us to be. Readers are given sound, doable tools for looking at God, His provisions, and the principles He has established that enable them to walk in His way"—Provided by publisher.
    Includes bibliographical references.
    ISBN-13: 978-0-7642-0173-8 (hardcover : alk. paper)
    ISBN-10: 0-7642-0173-5 (hardcover : alk. paper)
    1. Christian life. I. Title.
    BV4501.3.S53155   2007
    248.4—dc22   2006036178

D U T C H   S H E E T S

is an internationally known
conference speaker, pastor, and
author. He has written many
books, including bestsellers
Intercessory Prayer and *How to
Pray for Lost Loved Ones.* Dutch
is the senior pastor of Freedom
Church in Colorado Springs,
Colorado. Dutch and his wife,
Ceci, their two daughters, and
three dogs make their home at
the base of the Rocky
Mountains.

CONTENTS

PART I

THE PROBLEM

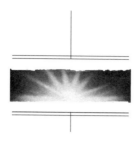

THE BREAK
HEARD 'ROUND
THE WORLD

It was a moment few football fans will ever forget. And for those watching the *Monday Night* game as I was on November 18, 1985, it's an image we'll never shake.

The lights of RFK Stadium were shining brightly as the 5–5 Washington Redskins hosted the 7–3 New York Giants. Into the second quarter, star quarterback Joe Theismann had the hot hand, having completed seven of his first ten passes. Coach Joe Gibbs, sensing momentum, signaled in a trick play: a flea-flicker. Theismann handed off to his veteran back, John Riggins, who rushed toward the line; before being tackled, Riggins tossed the ball back to Theismann, who surveyed the field for an open receiver.

Not that he could've done anything if he'd found one. Hall-of-Famer Lawrence Taylor, one of football's most feared defenders, had instantly sniffed out the ruse, steamrolled into the backfield, and knocked teammate Harry Carson into the QB. What followed was no normal sack. In one of the most wince-inducing, stomach-turning moments in sports history, Theismann's right leg snapped in two; his tibia suffered an open fracture, and his broken fibula tore through his skin. To this day, players on both sides recall hearing what sounded like the firing of a shotgun. The crowd hushed to a near silence. As those on the field quickly backed away, everyone watching saw the grotesque, hideous image of bone protruding from sock.

That one play ultimately ended Theismann's illustrious career. "I felt like it was just a broken leg," he recalls, adding that he'd broken his leg years before and returned to the field only two months later. Yet this

> **YOU DON'T HAVE TO BE A FOOTBALL FAN TO KNOW IT TAKES MORE THAN A BANDAGE AND IODINE TO FIX A COMPOUND FRACTURE.**

time the lasting damage was obvious. When he attempted comeback after comeback over the next two years, teams would take one look at his restricted mobility and turn him down. No matter how hard he tried, he couldn't return to his original condition.[1]

DOWN FOR THE COUNT

I've broken an arm, finger, little toe (yes, little toe), and nose—perhaps just enough to empathize somewhat with the complications and potential frustrations of the healing process. You don't have to be a football fan to know it takes more than a bandage and iodine to fix a compound fracture. The bone is set and placed in a cast, and doctors have to monitor its condition. If it's not corrected right away, it can heal crookedly; eventually it won't be able to bear weight, and over the long haul, may become entirely useless.

How many of us have felt the same way in our efforts to follow God? We asked Jesus into our heart and everything seemed different. The world went from a few muddy colors to high-resolution, high-definition vibrancy. The Word was jumping off the page at us, and His presence seemed to be everywhere we looked.

Then we got sacked. And something got broken.

A sudden job loss revealed our lack of faith. A divorce mangled our self-worth and made us wonder if we could ever trust again. An unresisted temptation began an addiction to Internet pornography. An unkind comment resurrected our suppressed bitterness toward a parent. Or a long-term struggle we thought would simply vanish when we embraced Christ suddenly re-reared its ugly head. Whatever single event or ongoing condition shook us out of our comfort zone, we began walking with a spiritual limp. Like a "good Christian," we immediately ran a self-diagnosis, searched our Bible for a prescriptive quick-fix verse, and prayed hard that we'd never break in the same place again.

But then we did. Again. And again. And again. Maybe we even had people lay hands on us, intercede for us, or act as our accountability partners. And yet after the five-hundredth time of giving in, it felt like we had no strength left to fight. We were ineffective in duking it out with the foaming anger that ran rampant. We felt weak in battling our lust. We succumbed to overeating. A negative self-image kept us trapped in the maze of fear, insecurity, and despair. And, eventually, we felt like a hopeless cause—an inept, ineffective Christian.

Naturally, it's in this stage that the nagging questions begin—questions that seem so unspiritual and disloyal to our newfound God and His Word. But questions that, nonetheless, *are* there and begin to eat away at our confidence and well-being. What happened? Why can't we seem to overcome our strongholds, much less our "petty" daily sins? Why is it so difficult to be truly free? Why are we perpetually broken? And why does it seem there are so many of us struggling just to get by?

Why didn't the lustful thoughts go away? Why didn't the desire for narcotics leave? Why should we even need a bumper sticker that says, "Christians aren't perfect, just forgiven"? Aren't we supposed to be the ones who walk in victory over sin? Didn't Christ, through His sacrifice, already take care of our weaknesses? Matthew 8:17 says He did:

> He Himself took our weaknesses and carried our diseases. (HCSB [from Isaiah 53:4])

I remember the frustration I felt while sitting across from a sobbing, frighteningly thin young girl caught in the awful web of anorexia. I just couldn't harmonize my theology with her experience. She was a Christian. She didn't want to die. She truly wanted to be free of her problem—at least a deep part of her did.

Then there are the many believers I've known or spoken with who've yielded to sexual temptation and paid dear prices. I recall one leader who fell prey to homosexual behavior and lost everything—his marriage, his career, and eventually his life to AIDS. His mindset wasn't the typical rationalizing, justifying, God-made-me-this-way attitude. He wept bitter tears, claiming that he wanted to be free but at times couldn't seem to stop himself. I *knew* him. I cried with him. No one will ever convince me he wasn't sincere in his desire for freedom.

You've known some. Maybe you stare at one every day in the mirror. The issues have different names, but the question is the same: *Why* can't we seem to overcome?

This is what *Roll Away Your Stone* is all about: finding a full, lasting solution. Throughout history God has always provided a way to overcome. He is the Great Physician and deliverer. And despite your frustrations with what you thought was His way to fix your problem—turns out, it wasn't—His solution brings complete, *permanent* results. If you're reading this and aren't yet experiencing true victory and freedom, somewhere along the line something in you hasn't been completely restored to the way God intended.

Obviously, breaking a bone isn't natural. It changes the nature of how things are supposed to be—namely, that the bone remains straight, intact, and connected to the rest of the body. A break sets things on another course.

The same is true for your life. God did not intend for you to live a defeated existence that always loses its battles with sin, character flaws,

> **GOD DID NOT INTEND FOR YOU TO LIVE A DEFEATED EXISTENCE THAT ALWAYS LOSES ITS BATTLES.**

or debilitating wounds. His love and forgiveness *are* always available, but He doesn't accept you in your broken state just for the sake of having you be a permanent fixer-upper. He wants you healed, restored, and free! He wants you back in your original form, the way He created you.

THE QUESTIONS NO ONE WANTS TO ASK (OR ANSWER)

I learned this while at my wit's end. It was 1977, I was attending Christ for the Nations in Dallas, and my ongoing struggles with fear, insecurity, and jealousy had left me feeling frustrated and defeated. Like most Christians, I identified with Paul's words in Romans 7:15:

> What I am doing, I do not understand; for I am not practicing what I would like to do, but I am doing the very thing I hate.

I wasn't a new believer. I'd experienced God in powerful ways. I'd already seen Him do miraculous things both in me and in others around me. I wasn't battling overwhelming demons or life-threatening addictions, but still I knew there had to be something more, some way out of this doomed cycle. *There had to be a provision for true freedom.*

"If the Son makes you free, you will be free indeed" (John 8:36) . . . right? Surely God didn't want my life to amount to nothing more than a series of ups and downs. If Jesus had come to conquer sin, could I not do the same by His power? Though I understood Paul's sentiment, the entirety of Romans 7 only left me more confused.

Turns out I wasn't the only guy.

> Martin Luther was one who struggled with his sins. Before his break with the Catholic church he went to confession every day and was so guilt-ridden by his sins he would almost have gone every hour. On most nights Luther slept well, but he even felt guilty about that, thinking, "Here I am, sinful as I am, having a good night's sleep." So he would confess that. One day the older priest to whom Luther went for confession said to him, "Martin, either find a new sin and commit it, or quit coming to see me!"[2]

We know the end of the story. Luther became the catalyst that changed the direction of the church and has reverberated through half a millennium. He didn't find a new sin—he discovered a radical, permanent solution in the form of God's grace. That's what I want for you—a radical, permanent solution! So does God.

But I'm not speaking only to those struggling with a character flaw, a habitual sin, a seemingly indefatigable addiction, or a wound from the past that just won't heal. I want to go beyond our obvious problems and look at some of the more subtle issues we should be considering, the ones we hide behind a Christian façade.

- Why do I grapple with faith?
- Why can't I overcome my trust issues?
- Why am I so selfish at times?
- Why, if I'm promised perfect peace, do certain fears seem to have such a grip on me?
- If God's Spirit lives in me, why is it so difficult to connect with Him and hear His voice?
- Why do I struggle with pride? Unforgiveness? Rage? Bitterness? Lack of discipline? Envy? Overeating?

I don't want to depress you. I just think it's time for us to get real, to get honest with ourselves. The unbelievers around us already have—they ask these questions about us. I'm sorry to be so blunt, but that's why many of them don't want our Jesus—they wonder, *What difference would He make?*

I've asked myself these questions, and I've asked them of God. I've also spent countless hours looking for answers, and I believe I've uncovered some. This isn't a book about psychology or counseling, and it isn't a self-help pep talk. It does offer substantive solutions needed to set you on a new course, to start you on an enjoyable and fascinating journey. (And it *is* a journey; there's no way to find or apply all the answers in three or four days, or three or four chapters.) And to be honest, some of it may be a bit painful. But as with corrective surgery that helps us heal, we can find that what's a bit painful can hurt so good!

On this endeavor into the oft-forbidden realm of questioning our inconsistencies, we'll attempt to do what cynical secularists, humanists, and godless psychology cannot: truly understand humankind's need. Contrary to many of their beliefs, the created cannot look to itself for definition; this understanding is found only in its Creator. When the source of life is denied, the reason for life and the design of life are lost, the answers excluded before the queries are made. There is, therefore, no finish line—just a race. No answers, only questions. We, on the other hand, will look to the Source of Life, the Creator, in order to understand ourselves, the created.

The Reality of Freedom

Jesus' statement in John 8:36 is powerful: We can be "free indeed." We'll later tackle this in greater detail, but for now it's important that we agree upon what being *truly* free looks like. Christ wasn't talking about a partial freedom, nor was He suggesting a short-lived temporary liberty. He was speaking of a true, complete, and lasting freedom.

The Greek word Jesus used for "indeed" is *ontôs*, which means "really," or "actually."[3] It denotes a real existence; in other words, it is reality. In one of its few New Testament occurrences, *ontôs* is employed to describe the resurrection: the disciples announced, "The Lord has risen *indeed*"! (Luke 24:34 ESV).[4] It wasn't just a spiritual resurrection, something occurring only in the invisible, heavenly realm—there was a literal, real, actual resurrection of Christ's body. The *New Living Translation* says, "The Lord has really risen!" He *is* risen, in reality! The stone was rolled away from His tomb, and the risen Jesus stepped out as the conqueror of sin, death, weakness, and pain. Forever, really risen.

God wants to roll away your stone as well. He wants you just as free as Jesus is risen—Christ's death and resurrection were for you. God's intent is to so saturate our lives with His Life and Spirit that our everyday existence embodies and expresses the victorious and death-conquering resurrection of His Son.

I know you would like that. I too enjoy living in reality rather than in a fantasy-based, über-spiritual world. I don't want simply to confess that I'm free, that I'm righteous, that I'm holy, that I'm an overcomer; I want to actually live out those realities. I don't want my stated or legal standing in Christ to be one thing and my experience to be something else altogether. Yet no honest Christian contends that his walk always mirrors the biblical promises. At some point, we must be honest enough to acknowledge this and ask why it's true.

Rest assured: Your experience *can*, in an ever-increasing way, match your spiritual standing in Christ. I have found that for this to occur, we must have a true knowledge of three basics.

> **YOUR EXPERIENCE *CAN*, IN AN EVER-INCREASING WAY, MATCH YOUR SPIRITUAL STANDING IN CHRIST.**

(1) We Must Know Ourselves   Who are we? Why do we do the things we do? Why does one part of us so desperately desire to change, to become more disciplined, to walk in freedom, while another part of our make-up sometimes (or often) trumps this desire? Why does it seem so easy for some believers to overcome, to walk in faith, to hear God's voice while others cannot? Is this because of strongholds; and if so, what are they exactly and how do they work? Bottom line: We can't fix something before we know how it's composed and how it functions. In order to be restored to all that God originally intended for us, we must understand how He made us.

Unfortunately, our purpose and understanding of ourselves have become self-defined rather than God-defined. We've digressed in our relativistic society to a belief that there really is no problem, and if there is ... well, it's *your* problem, certainly not mine. Make no mistake: The Lord perfectly understands "the problem," and He's made this clear to us through His written Word. He hasn't forgotten the severe break we suffered at the fall, and He also knows the importance of our coming to grips with that broken state. This is exactly what we'll examine in this book's initial chapters. Many lights will come on in your mind and heart as you begin to truly understand yourself.

(2) *We Must Know Our Enemy* Along with understanding our composition, we have to recognize adversarial efforts that keep us bound or anemic. How does Satan work against us? How does he use our fleshly nature? What methods does he employ on the carnal mind? In what ways does Adam's fall affect us? How does he control us through our past?

There's nothing more disheartening than a Christian blindsided by the devil. And yet it happens all the time. Several years ago spiritual warfare suddenly became all the rage among believers; everyone and his dog were reading books about angels, demons, and principalities. At least among charismatics, almost every worship service raised a battle cry to tear down enemy walls. Yet how many victories over Satan's strategies were really achieved?

If you know anything about me, you know I wholeheartedly affirm the need for spiritual warfare (see 2 Corinthians 10:3–5). But it's not enough simply to recognize the enemy's existence or to be conscious of his presence in this world; we must be aware of his strategies, because to the degree we are ignorant of his schemes, to that degree he will take advantage of us (2 Corinthians 2:11). We'll tackle this as we consider the lies he's used to keep us shackled to our problematic nature. Though this is not a book on demons, I do want to expose their tactics (which often center on how they use *us*).

(3) *We Must Know Our God and Know His Provision for Us* God reveals truth to us. His Word establishes the ground on which our life must stand. So when it comes to being an overcomer, what are the solutions He offers to affect our situation? What does He present as an answer? We have to know more than "Jesus is the answer," as true as this is. For application to our everyday

life, we must know the specific principles God communicates to us through His Word.

Thankfully, God absolutely provided our solution. This book's second and third parts show practical ways we can apply His heaven-sent answer.

Set for Fullness

No one wants to be called ineffective. Hopeless. Unsuccessful. Fruitless. Especially not when it comes to being a follower of Christ. But the sad fact is, so many of us have resigned ourselves to coexisting with lifelong shortcomings. Our limp has remained a lasting fixture as we've made peace with paralysis and believed the lie that our best-case plight is to hobble through one futile struggle after another. From there, we present a false-front image, project a plastic smile, and when we feel ashamed, hope we can muster a little more strength to try just a little bit harder. Having thrown in the towel, we've settled for "survive" when God wants us to "THRIVE."

Let me announce to you that there is an end to this cycle. God's original plan for your life—a victorious life of freedom, joy, and kingdom purpose—can be reinstated. Your brokenness can be "set" for permanent healing.

Plan to get well instead of seeking an early retirement from God's purposes for you. Follow the example of onetime inmate Charles Dutton.

> No one imagined Dutton would ever amount to any-thing, for he spent many years imprisoned for man-slaughter. When asked how he managed to make such a remarkable transition, this now-successful Broadway star replied, "Unlike the other prisoners, I never deco-rated my cell."[5]

It's time for your incarceration to end. You're headed for complete freedom. If you've decorated your cell, take everything down—NOW. You *can* be free.

On Resurrection Day, "a severe earthquake had occurred, for an angel of the Lord descended from heaven and came and rolled away the stone and sat upon it. And his appearance was like lightning . . ." (Matthew 28:2–3). Don't you just love that—the angel sat on the stone. God doesn't like things that imprison His sons and daughters. He sends earthquakes, angels—whatever it takes—to move them out of the way.

Get ready to step into the brilliant light of a new day and breathe the exhilarating air of freedom.

And as we begin our journey toward restoring the reality of God's original intent for us, allow me to be the first to congratulate you on your destiny: joining the ranks of the risen.

STANDING ON THE PROMISES ... AND THEN FALLING OFF

But you *promised!*"

I was pleading with my dad, using what I thought was my razor-sharp twelve-year-old logic against his bleary-eyed thirty-two-year-old rationale. Surely he would yield. Surely I could wear him down. Surely he'd consent to buying me the new bicycle.

Dad had promised my brother and me new bikes but hadn't come through. We clearly remembered his having gone to the shop with us, standing to the side as we ran around like ballistic puppies and hopped on every bike in the place. "This one, Dad! *This* is the one I want ... no, no wait, *this* one!"

With each freshly painted, glossy ride I sat on, I envisioned racing down neighborhood sidewalks, wind whizzing in my ears, the world a fuzzy blur in my wake. All the bikes were attached to a rail that prevented actually riding in the store. But I just knew the Blue Rider 3000 (the one I finally decided on) would take me to streets untold, at speeds unimagined. Surely Dad could see that *this* was what I really needed for the summer.

Noticing my uncontrolled exhilaration at finding "The One," my father came over to check out the extraordinary specimen of factory-assembled art. "Yep, you're right," he said with an earnest nod, never taking his eyes from it. "That's a fine-lookin' bike. Maybe your mother and I could think about someday getting it for you . . . you know, with your birthday coming up and all."

He'd said the magic words. My birthday was around the corner, and my brother's followed later in the year (he, too, had picked out his dream two-wheeler). To me it was as good as a done deal. Without precisely saying so, Dad had essentially promised us each the birthday present to top all birthday presents.

When There's Pain With Promises

A promise is a universally accepted verbal token of remembrance. It's a pledge that what you say will come to pass, an oath that commits your guarantee to a future time. If that promise never comes to fruition, then, for someone, a notch gets etched on the "untrustworthy" tally.

For a child, in particular, there's nothing worse than an unfulfilled promise. It scars the heart and taints the memory. When my dad didn't get me the bike, I felt devastated. However, the problem *wasn't* Dad's inability to stay true to his word. It was my inability to see things from his wiser point of view. The bikes, which came at Christmas, were a great sacrifice for Mom and Dad, considering his meager salary. Looking back, the ordeal proved that he understood something I had yet to grasp: Timing matters.

Painful lesson for a kid to learn. We want things to work out our way, and sooner rather than later (or as often as not, *now*). But honestly, is it any different as an adult? If anything, we grown-ups demand things even faster and more catered to our desires. We want a microwavable God, an instant-mix faith, and on-demand answers. And when it comes to dealing with divine promises—at least those that seem unfulfilled—we can quickly revert back to childish ways.

- ✎ "God promised me He'd bring me a husband . . . but I haven't even met anyone. I've given up on His sending a man my way. I'll find one on my own."

- ✎ "God told me when I started this business that it would be a prosperous venture, but I'm barely scraping by. He's not coming through, so I'm not tithing. If He's not willing to help me out, why should I help Him?"

- ✎ "God pledged He would be near to the brokenhearted, that He would 'have compassion on His afflicted.' but I suffered abuse years ago and am still struggling with major self-worth issues—to the point of sometimes having suicidal thoughts. If He won't make himself real to me, what's the point in fighting all this?"

To some degree, we've all felt slighted by God's timing, whether or not we've acknowledged it; most of us have questioned either our ability to hear His voice or His ability to answer (or both). In the last chapter we asked some hard questions related to why our experiences don't always harmonize with scriptural promises. Let's turn back to examine some of those assertions.

What about the more sweeping pledges the Word offers to every believer? You know, the basic promises we learned on Day One of becoming a Christian, like 2 Corinthians 5:17: "If anyone is in Christ, he is a new creature; the old things passed away; behold, new things have come." How many of us quickly discovered after we were saved that we weren't *completely* new? That our "old things," rather than being entirely gone, still bothered us from time to time? That *some* things hadn't changed one bit?

WHAT GIVES?

After recommitting my life to Christ in 1973, I still grappled with old patterns of the flesh. I remember an agonizing conversation with God that was held late one night while sitting on the hood of my car. I was devastated that my life experiences were not matching matter-of-fact scriptural promises. I was having trouble overcoming some of my old habits and cravings. Lust was a big one.

HOW MANY OF US QUICKLY DISCOVERED AFTER WE WERE SAVED THAT WE WEREN'T COMPLETELY NEW?

I was also facing major heart issues like jealousy, anger, insecurity, and bitterness. As I mentioned before, my frustration grew every time I ended up doing the things I didn't want to do. I was confused over how God could say one thing in the Bible, yet I never saw it actually happen in my life. For instance, I'd read that God "always leads us in triumph in Christ" (2 Corinthians 2:14). *Always?* Sounded great to me, but the reality was, I didn't always triumph—in fact, many times I got triumphed *over*.

Another verse in 2 Corinthians says that "all the promises of God in Him [Christ] are Yes, and in Him Amen, to the glory of God through us" (1:20 NKJV). Yes and Amen. How many promises? *All* of them. I'll be honest: they don't always work out that way for me. I can't remember the last time I was receiving all God's promises. How about you? Almost seems to me the verse should say, "Some of God's promises are Yes and Amen; others are hit-and-miss in Christ Jesus."

Don't you just want to be blunt with God sometimes? *What in the world are You talking about? How do You explain this one?* I'm simply being forthright about my experiences, and perhaps they're like yours. I don't mean to offend you, and in my heart I do know that God's Word is true. But isn't it right for me, as a pastor and spiritual leader, to say these things and acknowledge their impact on me rather than pretending I have no connection to them? We must be truthful, and remember, God already knows us exactly as we are. Our honesty may surprise us, but it doesn't at all take Him by storm.

At times the Bible can *seem* downright contradictory. Again, let's be authentic: let's admit that our experiences don't always match up with what we read in God's Word. Romans 8:37 says, "In all these things we overwhelmingly conquer through Him who loved us." The difficult-to-translate Greek word used for "overwhelmingly conquer" basically means "abundantly conquering," to be a "super-conqueror."[1] So I'm an overcomer—and then some. We not only win, we *always* win ... and we win with something left over. We're super-conquerors in God to the *n*th degree! We're never defeated! We can't be stopped!

Hmm. Have you found that to be the case? I know I haven't. I've lost more than my share of battles to worry, fear, unbelief, discontent, lustful thoughts ... and I'll bet you have too. And yet God matter-of-factly says we're all "more than conquerors."

Case closed.

Doesn't Look So New to Me

At one point I joined the staff at my alma mater, Christ for the Nations, and on a certain day I found myself sitting across from a young woman who'd come to the school in search of freedom. I was visiting with her to see if I could help in any way.

I quickly realized I was out of my league. She stared down at the table the entire time, not once looking me straight in the eye, even though we carried on a decent conversation. Her history explained why.

She had been sexually abused throughout her childhood by her father, her brother, her uncles ... virtually every man in her family. Until she was thirteen or fourteen, her father—a deacon at their church—often made her sleep in the same bed with him. Her mother, meanwhile, was so afraid that she neither said nor did anything to stop the appalling atrocities. As a result, this young woman had one of the worst self-images I'd ever seen or even heard of. Despite being born again, she absolutely abhorred herself. Though several years had passed, she was still profoundly damaged.

Weren't all things supposed to be new for her the moment she invited Christ into her heart? Doesn't the promise say that "her old things" were to have passed away? How could I expect her to reconcile God's promises with her life when I, as a minister and Bible teacher, couldn't even do that for her?

Ultimately, the seemingly massive chasm between divine promises and human experiences can be boiled down to a single question:

If I am, why don't I?

Yes, that's an awkward phrasing. But it's true and accurate. If I am who God says I am, then why don't I act like it? We'll address this (and other related matters) before we're finished, but for the moment let's hone in and consider the essence of our dilemma as we learn to be truly honest with ourselves.

A Pat on the Head Won't Cut It

Winston Churchill once said, "The truth is incontrovertible; malice may attack it, ignorance may deride it, but in the end, there it is."[2]

He was right. Unfortunately, rather than admitting we're not understanding why things don't add up, too often we revert to "Christianese" and spout the pat answers we've all heard in response to the tough questions no one dares ask. When we *do* dare, here are some of the answers we get:

- "You'll be okay. You just need to grow and mature as a Christian." (Maybe that's true, but it does nothing for us when we're facing a seemingly irreconcilable situation. And actually, some Christians never mature past certain problems. It's a cop-out response.)

- "You just need to get your mind renewed." (Good point. True, the mind must be transformed by the Holy Spirit. But that answer is far too simplistic; mind renewal is a lifelong process, not a one-shot deal. I can't imagine saying that to the young lady at Christ for the Nations.)

- "You just need the baptism of the Holy Spirit." (I can't begin to tell you how many times I've heard people say this. In charismatic and Pentecostal circles, we're quick with this line when someone's struggling with habitual sin, ongoing setbacks, a faulty mindset, or something from the past. However, I've seen countless supposedly Spirit-baptized people who spoke in tongues, prophesied, and did all the things on the "Spirit-filled list," yet were undeniably more carnal than some who had not satisfied these "qualifications." Likewise, believers who don't speak in tongues can be far more mature and free than some who do. In my experience, this baptism isn't what cures someone.)

- "You just need more faith." (Been there, done that. In fact, I was first in line at the faith camp for a time. And while faith is always an issue, firing this at someone needing help and hope doesn't offer much help or yield much hope.)

- "You need to deny self." Or "You ought to crucify your flesh." Huh? What's that supposed to mean to a new Christian? Or, better yet, my least favorite, "You just need to get sanctified." (I understand the meaning of these, having been in the ministry for years. But they're easily misconstrued, and using these lines on a new believer shows how ineffective they are.)

Other contrived answers can cause even more serious damage, especially for young Christians:

- "If you really wanted to change, you could."

➤ "If you really want to stop doing that, why don't you? You have free will."

And the most destructive response I've encountered, usually delivered with spiritual haughtiness:

➤ "Well, then, you must not really be saved, because my Bible says if anyone is in Christ, he is a new creation. Old things are passed away. All things are new. If that isn't your experience, you must not really be born again."

Makes me want to smack them—*with* my Bible! (I'm still working on the "turn the other cheek" verse, myself.) I've watched people walk away from their faith because of irresponsible and vicious comments like these. They are truly devastating.

Neither Instantaneous Nor Accidental

The simple truth is—and here is what so many Christians don't realize: *The promises and assertions of Scripture aren't automatic for believers.* Though they are legally true and valid, they won't "just happen" or naturally slip into place, no matter how adamantly we welcome them, recite them, or pray them. Sure, in this way you may stumble onto some truth and taste a bit of freedom. And over time, you may even shed some of your old self, some of your old struggles. But I assure you it won't be simply because you've become a Christian.

Freedom isn't an instant or automatic reality just because you're saved. As Vice-President Adlai Stevenson once said, "We have confused the free with the free and easy."[3] I've known people who've been believers for a half century who in some areas aren't an ounce freer than the day they met Jesus. A Christian *can* remain full of pride, selfishness, fear, greed, or fury. I guarantee that if a stronghold is strong enough in your life, you won't simply grow out of your shackles and into newness.

There are certain principles that must be put in motion for us to see the fulfillment of God's promises. No matter how this sounds, it isn't legal-

FREEDOM ISN'T AN INSTANT OR AUTOMATIC REALITY JUST BECAUSE YOU'RE SAVED.

istic, and it isn't contrary to His grace. God's love and grace are unconditional; they're free, with no strings attached. His benefits and the fruit of our salvation, however, are not.

In chapter 1, I listed three truths we need to know in order to move into freedom: ourselves, our enemy, and our God and His provision. Here is an expansion of the third truth:

> To the degree that we (1) understand Christ's provision for us, (2) understand the principles governing that provision, and (3) appropriate them through obedience and faith—to that degree we will receive and walk in His provision for or promise to us.

(1) "To the degree that we understand Christ's provision for us . . ." This doesn't mean merely hearing about it or quoting a verse. It's a matter of truly understanding, of having real revelation. Usually when God's revelation comes, we "stumble" onto it. We'll be reading our Bibles or listening to a teaching and—boom!—insight hits us straightaway. Something clicks, and a whole new world opens up to us. That's awesome, but as we'll gradually see, we don't have to stumble upon revelation. We can receive it on purpose.

Fundamental to this life-changing revelation is understanding God's *ultimate* provision for us: salvation. But what exactly does it mean to be saved? What part of us is saved? What are we saved from? As we'll later discuss, this dimension is often poorly understood.

(2) *"To the degree that we understand the principles governing Christ's provision (or promise) . . ."* It isn't enough only to know that God has promised something to us; we must grasp what principles in His Word govern that provision. He's established standards, a code— "rules," if you will—and the entire Bible is based on them. Sowing and reaping. Dying and living. Becoming the least to be the greatest. Growing poor to become rich. Losing it all to gain everything. It's an ongoing issue of cause and effect. In His infinite wisdom, God created a universe that functions accordingly.

It's no different for our Christian walk. With every promise comes a condition that governs it. It may be put forward in a different verse, passage, book, or section. That's why it's crucial for us, the Lord's followers, to take the whole counsel of God, to understand the entire scope of His living, breathing Word.

The Herald and Presbyter, a nineteenth-century publication, ran a story about the importance of considering Scripture's entirety.

> A certain wayward young man ran away from home and was not heard of for years. In some way, hearing that his father had just died, he returned home and was kindly received by his mother. The day came for the reading of the will; the family all gathered together, and the lawyer began to read the document. To the surprise of all present, the will told in detail of the wayward career of the runaway son. The boy in anger arose, stamped out of the room, left the house, and again was not heard from for three years. When eventually he was found, he was informed that the will, after telling of his waywardness,

had gone on to bequeath him $15,000 [about $3 million by today's standards]. How much sorrow he would have saved himself and others if he'd only heard the reading through! Thus many people only half-read the Bible and turn from it dissatisfied. The Bible says, "The wages of sin is death," yes, but it says more; it says, "But the gift of God is eternal life."[+]

It's careless to hold tight to a divine promise without considering its conditions. That's like offering an "expert" critique on a movie when you've only seen the trailer. With each guarantee, until you discover the ruling principle, you'll never experience the promised fulfillment.

(3) "To the degree that we appropriate the provisions through obedience and faith . . ."

This isn't a case of either/or. We can't choose to be obedient yet lack faith, or vice versa. By obedience, I'm not only referring to obeying God's commands; obedience includes the implementation of the principles behind the commands. That means *doing* the Word: We must obey the Lord and do what He says, and we must also lay hold by faith.

What does this mean—lay hold by faith? It means seeing that the fruition of a God-promise can actually hinge upon *us*. That's downright blasphemy in certain circles, but Paul told Timothy to "fight the good fight of faith; take hold of the eternal life to which you were called" (1 Timothy 6:12). How many times, biblically, do we see the Lord either rewarding with or withholding His favor based on how a person follows His instructions?

Moses couldn't enter the Promised Land, for which he'd been waiting more than forty years, because he disobeyed God's orders (Numbers 20:9–12). His actions themselves seem like minor details, yet to the Lord, the heart issue involved was major. Samson's gift of extraordinary strength was taken away because he disobeyed God and told Delilah his secret, which ultimately led to his death (Judges 16). On the positive side, how can any believer forget Abraham's willingness to sacrifice his own son to the Lord—only to be blessed as the father of many nations (Genesis 22:1–18)?

Grace and mercy *are* at the very heart of our God. And yes, we don't earn our salvation through works, and we cannot merit the Lord's love through good deeds. Nonetheless, as I stated earlier, while God's love is unconditional, His benefits and the fruit of our salvation are not. We must lay hold of them through faith and action.

Nothing pleases the Lord more than an obedient heart brimming with faith: "To obey is better than sacrifice" (1 Samuel 15:22). Faith is often the mother of obedience, motivating us to do what the Father instructs.

> In the middle of the night, in a small Midwest farming community, the two-story home of a young family caught fire. Quickly everyone made their way through the smoke-filled house out into the front yard. Everyone except a five-year-old boy. The father looked up to the boy's room and saw his son crying at the window, rubbing his eyes.
>
> The father knew better than to reenter the house to rescue his son, so he yelled, "Son, jump! I'll catch you."
>
> Between sobs, the boy responded to the voice he knew so well. "But I can't see you."
>
> The father answered with great assurance. "No, son, you can't. But I can see you!" The boy jumped and was safe in his father's arms.[5]

That's the way faith works. It enables us to obey even when we don't understand or can't yet see the end result. And God loves faith—so much that He requires it. But how does faith grow in us to the point that we can lay hold of the promise? We will answer this question as we progress.

Though the promises of God are not automatic, they remain unfailingly true. No matter what *we* do, God cannot lie or offer anything false. Yet if we want to see His promises fulfilled in our own lives,

> **THOUGH THE PROMISES OF GOD ARE NOT AUTOMATIC, THEY REMAIN UNFAILINGLY TRUE.**

we're required to lay hold of them through faith and through obedience; just as faith is often the mother of obedience, so is revelation uncovered as we obey.

To the degree we follow through with these conditions—understanding the provision, knowing its governing principles, and properly fulfilling them—*to that degree we'll receive God's provision in our lives.* His promises will come through. His Word won't return void. We'll see the fulfillment of verse after verse after verse—just as He intended from the beginning.

On one occasion, two of Christ's closest friends questioned His timing and actions. Lazarus, the brother of Mary and Martha, had died. Both sisters knew Jesus could have healed Lazarus had He chosen to come when they sent for Him. Now it was too late.

> Martha therefore said to Jesus, "Lord if you had been here, my brother would not have died."
> Therefore, when Mary came where Jesus was, she saw Him and fell at His feet, saying to Him, "Lord, if You had been here, my brother would not have died" (John 11:21, 32).

But Christ wasn't late; He had another plan, far bigger than a healing. Though Lazarus had now been dead four days, Jesus approached the tomb and said, "Remove the stone" (John 11:39).

Appalled, Martha quickly interjected, "Lord, by this time there will be a stench . . ." (v. 39). Jesus, however, was not afraid of the odor of death; He knew the life in Him was stronger than the death in the tomb. And in one of the most dramatic accounts of Scripture Christ raised Lazarus from the dead.

You may think it is too late for your healing, that God simply hasn't and won't come through for you. Perhaps on the inside you feel the power of death is so strong you could never live.

But Jesus has other plans and is waiting with resurrection life to reverse the destructive power that has entombed you. His heart is the same today as it was two thousand years ago, and before He is finished you too will hear the words you've longed to hear: "Remove the stone!"

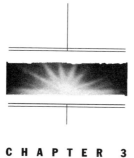

THE WAY WE WERE

Fourth-grade science class.

In between the spitballs flying across the room and the giggles erupting every time Mrs. Gregory uttered the words *sex* or *homo sapien*, I do remember learning a thing or two. Like the fact that a typical lightning bolt is hotter than the temperature of the sun's surface. Or that if the sun were the size of the dot on an ordinary-sized letter *i*, then our nearest star would be ten miles away.

But possibly nothing would be as impacting of and invaluable for my future years as the day we learned about water. H_2O. That marvelous sustainer of life that comes in various forms. Freeze it below 0 degrees Celsius, and it's as solid as a rock. (Just as painful too. I learned this when my friend Billy proved the solidity of ice by throwing a cube at my head.) Between 0 and 100 degrees Celsius, water's a liquid. And once it's past 100, say good-bye to its visibility as it turns into a gas. Each facet is independently unique yet part of the whole that makes up what we call water.

Fourth year of marriage.

Journeying along the highway of marital life, I was learning just how multifaceted my wife, Ceci, truly is. One forgotten anniversary of a special occasion and she could turn as cold as ice. Or one tender "I love you" from me in the morning and she was instantly a puddle of mushy love. And her ability to evaporate $100 bills on shopping trips astounded me to the point of producing steam. (I, of course, am never moody and never spend any of our hard-earned money.)

Just as I'd learned in fourth grade about water's composition and states, I came to discover that my wife is made up of several distinct "elements." She was prone to change forms, temperaments, and attitudes from time to time, and I quickly learned to distinguish which was which—and when I was allowed *ever so carefully* to add my input on those changes. (Men, you know *exactly* what I'm talking about.) Four years in, I'd gone through the routine of settling into everyday life with my mate while comprehending more about her than anyone else ever had. It didn't take long to understand and love each characteristic that was part of the entirety of Ceci, my wonderful wife.

A Three-for-One Deal

With everything multifaceted, God has a knack for making each individually essential. Think about it: What if water couldn't take a liquid form? Can you imagine what the atmosphere would be like if water never turned gaseous? And what would Ceci be without her remarkable talents for tracking down sales and saying just the right thing at just the right time? Every element is indispensable to making up the whole.

It was no different when God made humans. Adam, the prototype, was an amazing creation. God fashioned him "fearfully and wonderfully" (Psalm 139:14) "in His own image" (Genesis 1:27). Part of that likeness appears in the three distinct elements (just like God the Father, Son, and Spirit) that comprise our being: spirit, soul, and body (1 Thessalonians 5:23). I have entire books in my library that attempt to explain these three components of our makeup. That's not our purpose here, but a general understanding of each facet is important for our quest. To borrow the adage, we *did* become "broken," and we *do* need "fixing." The biblical word is *restored*, and we can't be restored to normalcy until we know what that is—and we humans have sure messed up "normal."

Before I say more about our three parts, let me give a brief heads up. You will see as we progress that I'm a teacher at heart and love word studies. I use them often to enhance, expand, and paint pictures. If you've not read one of my books before, please don't assume after a few definitions that I'm going to overwhelm you with dry, meaningless, technical jargon. That's not what I'm all about.

My readers generally find that the word studies are among the most beneficial parts of my writing. And beyond defining a word, I usually also give the Hebrew or Greek term. Many pastors, teachers, and others find them stimulating and helpful; if you don't need or want to examine an original word, I assure you it won't grow cumbersome or get in your way.

Having said this, there are seven Greek words I'll use repeatedly throughout this book. Eventually you'll know them well, and knowing them will help you recall and retain the truth they represent. For easy reference, here is the list:

(1) *pneuma:* "spirit"

(2) *pneumatikos:* "spirit-controlled"

(3) *psuché:* "soul"

(4) *psuchikos:* "soul-controlled"

(5) *zoé:* "God's life"

(6) *logos:* "word, logic, understanding"

(7) *alétheia:* "truth"

Don't worry about remembering all these right now; we'll get to their deeper meanings and discuss them below as we examine humanity's three "parts."

(1) *Spirit* Defining the term *spirit* can be difficult; it's often perceived to be a hazy concept. But for Christians, it need not be so hard, for this reason: The biblical Greek word for the human "spirit," *pneuma*, is the same word used for the Holy "Spirit." Accordingly, there is an implicit connection between God's Spirit and that of His human creation. Spirit is the part of our being that is God-like, or as the Scriptures state, was made in His "likeness" (Genesis 1:26). The Hebrew word for "likeness" means "comparable to."[1] At the creation, Adam's spirit was comparable to God's.

GOD DOES NOT COMMUNICATE WITH US FIRST THROUGH OUR MIND OR EMOTIONS BUT THROUGH OUR SPIRIT.

In regard to God dwelling in humans, the spirit is where, in us, He lives. Thus, *our spirit is the part of us that God intended to relate to Him and the spiritual realm in which He exists.* This is very important. God does not communicate with us first through our mind or emotions but through our spirit. *The spirit was what God intended to be dominant—in charge.* We were to be led and controlled by our spirit, which most scholars believe also houses our conscience and intuition. Spirit distinguishes us from the animal world.

(2) *Soul* Soul is the area we'll be dealing with most during these first few chapters because (A) it's the crux of where humanity veered from God's intended way and (B) it's the part of us that has become the problem. If you have issues, strongholds, or weaknesses, they're in

your soul. Though many people assume spirit and soul are one and the same, they are not. The Greek word for soul is *psuché*. Recognize a semblance of the word *psyche* in it? The psyche, or *psuché*, is the mind (intellect), emotions (feelings), and will (volition). Psychology, then, is the study of these three soul elements (usually with no thought given to the spirit). Here is the breakdown of these components:

- The mind (or intellect) reasons, thinks, forms logic, processes, and stores information.
- The emotions give us feelings, such as joy or sadness.
- The will (or volition), based on what we've put into our mind and emotions, makes the decisions—the will determines our course of action.

In essence, the soul is the processing mechanism, the computer mainframe, the translator. It is important to realize that the soul is *not* the part of

> **THE SOUL'S FUNCTION WAS NOT TO CONTROL OR LEAD US BUT TO SERVE OUR SPIRIT.**

us God intended to connect with and receive directly from the spiritual realm; our spirit was to do this and pass on the information to the soul, which would then process the information and store it. It could also receive and store information received through our body, through the five senses. Summary: *Adam's soul could receive and process information directly from the natural, physical, visible world around him; and from the spiritual, invisible realm, but only via the spirit.*

The soul's function was not to control or lead us but to serve our spirit:

> The spirit of man is the lamp of the Lord, searching all
> the innermost parts of his being. (Proverbs 20:27)

This made Adam a *pneumatikos*, a spiritually led and controlled man, not primarily a *psuchikos*, or soulishly controlled man (sometimes in Scripture translated "natural man"). Let me add a note about what some consider a separate element of our being: the heart. Many think that whenever the Bible mentions the spiritual heart, it's always referring to the spirit. Not true—sometimes it's referencing the spirit, sometimes the soul, and it can be difficult to determine which. At other times, I believe, it's referring to a combination of the two. *The spiritual heart is probably that unique inter-working of the soul and the spirit.*

(3) *Body* The body is exactly what it appears to be: our physical person, our flesh. Like the soul, *the body was made to relate to the natural world around us, the physical realm.* More important, it is the house in which our spirit and soul reside. Though it has its own hungers or appetites, it will basically obey the soul's commands.

A LIVING SOUL

Genesis 2:7 and 1 Corinthians 15:45 refer to man as a "living soul" (KJV). Your Bible version may use different wording, but the original text—in both Hebrew and Greek—literally translates this way. In Hebrew, we're called a *"chay nephesh,"* and in Greek, a *"zoé psuché."* Since the meaning is synonymous, we'll deal only with the latter.

Again, *psuché* means "soul" (mind, emotions, and will); *zoé*, a small but incredibly powerful term, in Scripture refers to the life of God. It represents the life-force that flows to us from God Himself.

Think back to when you first became a Christian. Remember the almost instant love, peace, hope, security, and more that washed over you when you asked Jesus into your heart? Like nothing you'd ever experienced, better than any mood-altering substance. That was the life of God actually entering into you. Eternal life. *Zoé.* It's the word always used when referring to the life we receive at salvation or conversion. Its Hebrew equivalent, *chay*, is also used to describe the Tree of Life in the garden of Eden.

Combining *zoé* with *psuché*, we get "living soul" or "life-filled soul." When God created Adam, He actually breathed His Spirit and life into him. Adam's spirit possessed God's eternal life, which then brought life to his soul and body. In other words, man's being came alive with the very life of God—*zoé*. And all because the Holy Spirit dwelled in Adam's spirit. The ramifications are almost staggering: *Adam was as much like God as he could possibly be without being God.* (See Genesis 1:26–28; Psalm 8:3–8.)

The Greek word for "spirit" (*pneuma*) is the exact same word for "breath." You could just as easily translate "Holy Spirit" as "Holy Breath." God's Holy Breath or Holy Spirit was placed in Adam, the pinnacle of His creation. So originally, man had God's *Pneuma* (Spirit) in his own *pneuma* (spirit). They were one; God's breath came into his. Job illustrated this when he said,

> The Spirit of God has made me, and the breath of the
> Almighty gives me life. (33:4)

God's life into Adam made him a living or "lifed" soul; they became spiritually entwined. Paul describes it this way: "The one who joins himself to the Lord is one spirit with Him" (1 Corinthians 6:17). *We were originally made to be joined with and to live by God's very life-giving breath.*

This also means God was Adam's motivating force; his existence, purpose, impetus—all the influences of life—sprang from God and His nature. Talk about an amazing creature! Adam was beyond anything most of us could fathom. Psalm 8:5 says he was made "a little lower than God," and that God "crown[ed] him with glory and majesty."

SERIOUS BRAINPOWER

Let's take a deeper look at the soul. It's vital to know, regarding Adam's soul (mind, emotions, and will), that he received his wisdom, understanding, and logic from God. From the moment God fashioned Adam from the dust of the earth, He began to inform and instruct him. Adam didn't need a written Bible; He had a talking Bible. God spoke with him personally! God's wisdom and logic were shared with him (not all of it, of course, but what God wanted him to know) through his spirit and then were stored in his soul (mind; *psuché*). And

> **GOD NEVER INTENDED THAT ADAM SHOULD FUNCTION INTELLECTUALLY APART FROM HIS INFLUENCE AND INSTRUCTION.**

here is a crucial point: *God never intended that Adam should function intellectually apart from His influence and instruction.* Adam was not made to be an independent thinker. (I don't want to jump ahead, but I must say that from this it's easy to see how messed up things have become.)

We can infer from the early passages of Genesis that God regularly came and talked with Adam. They were friends and family. As a result of this intimate relationship, God gave His favorite creation His own understanding—of life, creation, the laws of nature, Himself, etc. In the previous paragraph, in speaking of God's wisdom given to Adam, I used the word *logic* intentionally, because in the New Testament the "word" of God is linked to logic. "Word" is translated from *logos*, the same Greek word for logic. You can easily see our English word in this Greek word. Though *logos* includes written or spoken words, it also includes the message those words are communicating. This is why Jesus is called the *Logos*, the Word of God—He *is* God's message to us. Rather than the written Word, Adam had the Author, the Maker, personally sharing with him His *logos* (words of wisdom, understanding, logic).

Greek scholar Spiros Zodhiates defines *logos*, in the context of God's Word, as "God's reason or intelligence expressed in human speech."[2] I like this because it truly indicates who the *real* source of our intellect should be. I've known plenty of skeptics and cynics who wouldn't believe because they claimed that following God meant checking their mind at the front door. In their opinion, Christians are brainwashed robots following an ancient religion with no relevance to "real" life.

C. S. Lewis had plenty to say about that perspective:

> Anyone who is honestly trying to be a Christian will soon find his intelligence being sharpened: one of the reasons why it takes no special education to be a Christian is that Christianity is an education itself. That is why an uneducated believer like Bunyan was able to write a book [*The Pilgrim's Progress*] that has astonished the whole world.[3]

There is no greater teacher in the universe than God. And He was Adam's instructor in the ways of life. Through their spiritual connection, the Creator came and taught the created about creation. He imparted His own divine wisdom into the soul of a man.

This point is sufficiently significant to re-repeat: Man's understanding and logic were to come from God. *Again, God never intended that he function intellectually apart from His influence.* He was never to be an independent thinker, never to have independent knowledge. Never!

Our reasoning wasn't to be strictly human or natural; it was always meant to have a supernatural element. God's perfect creation—humankind—working in divine order, was to have every single element that traversed through the soul first filtered by the Spirit of God. *He* would be the origin of man's knowledge.

TRUTH'S AUTHOR

Another word for the God-based knowledge Adam's soul possessed is *truth* (Greek: *alétheia*). Biblically speaking, truth isn't just nuts-and-bolts information; facts aren't necessarily the same as spiritual truth, and knowledge in and of itself doesn't lead to biblical truth. For instance, Jesus said, "There is no truth in [the devil]" (John 8:44); Satan will sometimes dole out facts while completely missing or distorting the truth.

Truth—*alétheia*—literally means "the reality that existed in the original norm," or "the reality lying at the basis or essence of something." *Alétheia* is true and genuine reality.[4] With words like *reality*, *original*, *norm*, and *essence* defining truth, it becomes obvious that the Creator, God, is its Author.

There is no truth without God, since He created all reality. He is the basis for everything, the Originator. Is it any wonder, then, that the humanist argument, which denies the reality of God and places humans at the center, begins by attacking the very existence of truth? Humanist dogma asserts that everything is relative, that there is no absolute truth.

Think about it: Absolute truth necessitates the existence of an ultimate authority (which fallen man doesn't want). But if truth exists in an original form, then it didn't evolve from something else—it has a source. And so there must *be* a Source.

Stated more generally, if "reality" (truth) is the very "basis and essence," then there must be absolutes and an original source of those absolutes. But when the standard is denied or lost, as it is when God and His absolute truth is denied, anarchy is inevitable; the bar gets lowered until finally it's no longer even acknowledged as existing. *But truth does exist and can be summarized as the absolute standard, found in God, from which all wisdom, logic, and knowledge proceed. It has always existed in God, and it never changes.*

> When Lloyd C. Douglas, author of *The Robe* and other novels, was a university student, he lived in a boarding-house. Downstairs on the first floor was an elderly retired music teacher, now infirm and unable to leave the apartment.
>
> Douglas said that every morning they had a ritual. He would come down the steps, open the old man's door, and ask, "Well, what's the good news?"
>
> The old man would pick up his tuning fork, tap it on the side of his wheelchair, and say, "That's middle C! It was middle C yesterday; it will be middle C tomorrow; it will be middle C a thousand years from now. The tenor upstairs sings flat, the piano across the hall is out of tune, but, my friend, that is middle C!"[5]

There is a middle C. It exists today, and it always will. No refined data or trendy theories will eliminate it.

Likewise, there are absolutes. An absolute norm. An original. An *alétheia*. And ruling high above as the Creator of it all is God. The true God, who reigns in truth. This truth—the only truth—was available to Adam and was always to shape humankind's perspective.

The Original Spirit-Filled, Spirit-Led Guy

Adam was the perfect being, created by a perfect God to mirror Him. He literally was a presentation of God to this earth, even carrying around the Lord's glory.[6] In his spirit Adam had God's life (*zoê*) and breath (*pneuma*). In his soul he had God's Word (*logos*), which brought knowledge of God and an ability to comprehend truth (*alétheia*).

It's safe to say that with this format Adam didn't have to strain hard to hear God's voice; he didn't struggle to relate. There was a natural communion, led by God's Spirit living inside the man. From this perspective his soul could relate to his natural surroundings. Every thought process, every system of logic, every aspect of his rationality . . . it all came to him from God.

As a perfect being, Adam's spirit and soul worked in complete harmony, just as God intended. The spirit controlled and the soul carried out its bidding through the body. The spirit was the master, the soul served the spirit, and the body served the soul (and therefore, the spirit). Again, this made Adam a "spiritual man," a *pneumatikos* (1 Corinthians 2:13–14), which means he was ruled and motivated from his spirit—a spiritually controlled person. He had "the fruit of the spirit" (Galatians 5:22–23), which wouldn't have needed to be called the fruit of the *Holy* Spirit, for there was no difference. What flowed out of his spirit was being supplied by God's Spirit; God and man were entwined.

> **THE BIBLICAL DEFINITION OF A SPIRITUAL PERSON IS ONE WHO LIVES ACCORDING TO HIS SPIRIT INSTEAD OF HIS BODY OR SOUL.**

Today we erroneously classify a "spiritual person" according to how much Scripture he can quote, how intense his prayers are, how long he's been saved. In certain circles it's a matter of how well you prophesy or speak for God. Even outside church walls the world calls people "spiritual" based upon their devotion to religious practices. None of these makes a person truly spiritual: The biblical definition of a spiritual person is one who lives according to—is led by—his spirit instead of his body or soul.

Through his spirit, Adam—and then Eve as well—fellowshipped easily with God. Genesis 3:8 says Adam would hear God's voice in Eden in the cool of the day. *Cool* is the same word as "wind" or "breath"; I believe this "voice" in the "wind" probably refers to the Holy Spirit. That's how in tune were Adam and his Maker.

When the voice "blew" into the garden, Adam heard it clearly and accurately as that of his Creator. God talked with him. Their fellowship was sweet, natural, and easy. Because Adam's soul heard distinctly and effortlessly what his spirit communicated, the perfect man walked in perfect peace and perfect contentment. Everything was in perfect balance.

Not a bad setup for humanity. And it's how things always should have been. But then . . .

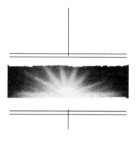

CHAPTER 4

"HEAVEN, WE HAVE A PROBLEM"

M ount Vesuvius erupts in AD 79, burying the entire city of Pompeii, Italy, and its residents in volcanic ash.

In the fourteenth century, the Black Death pandemic spreads throughout Europe, Asia, and the Middle East, killing more than twenty million people.

The Irish Potato Famine, lasting from 1845 to 1849, leads to as many as one million deaths.

The Spanish Flu of 1914, considered history's deadliest epidemic, causes anywhere from fifty to one hundred million fatalities, worldwide, in one year.

An earthquake, 8.2 on the Richter scale, hits Tangshan, China, in 1976; the death toll is estimated to be around five hundred thousand.

As millions watch around the globe, in 1986, the space shuttle *Challenger* explodes shortly after liftoff and claims the lives of all seven crew members.

On September 11, 2001, terrorist hijackings of four passenger jets lead to almost three thousand deaths at the World Trade Center, the Pentagon, and in Somerset County, Pennsylvania.

In 2004, a series of Indian Ocean tsunamis, originating from one of the most severe earthquakes ever recorded, kill almost two hundred thousand.

Had enough?

This brief list only scratches the surface of the planet's greatest natural and man-made disasters. It's heart-wrenching to imagine what the victims and their families endured. Yet all these catastrophes combined still don't measure up to the ruin brought upon this earth as a result of one man's wrong choice. In fact, his blunder caused it all. Every murder, death, rape, pain, disease—you fill in the blank—they all flow from Adam's rebellion.

He botched it. Big time. It's nearly impossible to state in human terms the fullness of the catastrophe that transpired. (Though Eve played a major role in the fall, God attributes primary responsibility to Adam, so I refer mainly to him in this discussion.)

God had created a perfect being that had His own life and breath, His own logic, and His own knowledge. But that wasn't enough for Adam. The only standard God established—"From the tree of the knowledge of good and evil you shall not eat" (Genesis 2:17)—Adam chose to disregard and defy.

Though I don't think it is possible to fully describe the catastrophe of the fall, I'll attempt at least a partial description of what occurred. I want to warn you in advance that it isn't pretty. We'll begin with the big picture and then get more detailed through the remainder of the chapter. Keep in mind that what happened to Adam was passed down to all of us.

> If by the transgression of the one, death reigned through the one . . . then as through one transgression there resulted condemnation to all men . . . as through the one man's disobedience the many were made sinners. (Romans 5:17–19)

- Adam is now disconnected from his life-source. He will look within himself for life's origin and meaning. Purpose will no longer be found in his Creator; he'll seek it on his own, eventually even denying the existence of a creator.

- Adam has exalted himself above God. Pride—the pleasing and preserving of self—will now be his ultimate driving force.

- Adam's desires and appetites have lost their governor. Their legitimate hungers will no longer have God-given parameters. He'll explore and experiment—all in the name of freedom—and when he tastes of life outside the boundaries of legitimacy, his wanderlust will only increase. Constraint has been lost.

- In Adam's mind he now knows more than God. His entire system of learning, of processing information and turning it into logic, has been turned upside down and is out of order. He'll now do these things from within—with his own cognitive abilities—based on trial and error and human reasoning. Everything will be based on information (what he can discover), not revelation (what God can reveal). It will flow from his natural world, not the spiritual realm. Logic will be human-born, human-centered—humanistic.

- Since he's on a quest for knowledge and wisdom, and since these will always be progressing and unfolding, Adam will claim there is no absolute truth—all is relative and constantly changing. He'll refuse to accept a standard and will move the bar to fit the situation or the day in which he lives. He'll make his own laws. And since to him truth is now relative, he'll be able to justify anything and everything.

- Adam is now a person controlled by the *psuché*—what Scripture calls a *psuchikos*, a "natural man" operating from the soul. He is no longer a *pneumatikos* (spirit-controlled and spirit-led person). He relates primarily to the natural realm; he will struggle with faith and with hearing God's voice. In short, if he can't see it, feel it, naturally prove it, and so forth, he'll have difficulty believing in or relating to it.

- That which was made to serve God and the spirit is now in complete rebellion and in complete control. God's

great challenge concerning Adam's redemption will not
be forgiving him but saving and taming his soul.

Make no mistake about it, whatever your weakness, sin, addiction,
controlling wound, un-Christlike attitude—whatever the issue in your
life that doesn't align with Scripture—the problem originates in your
soul.

What a mess! That's the big picture. Now let's break this down
and elaborate on the details.

> **OUR SOUL'S PRIMARY PURPOSE WAS TO SERVE OUR SPIRIT AND ENABLE US TO RELATE TO THE NATURAL, PHYSICAL WORLD.**

Remember, God created us to be led and dominated by our spirit. With His Spirit leading and guiding us on all matters of knowledge, logic, and reasoning, our soul's primary purpose was to serve our spirit and enable us to relate to the natural, physical world. This connection to the world around us was never intended to be the primary focus of our existence.

And yet with one decision Adam chose to elevate both his desires
and his own knowledge above God's. Knowledge, even of good versus
evil, wasn't the problem. It was that now Adam would have his own,
not God's. He and Eve couldn't restrain themselves from going after
what felt good for the moment, from taking the bait of having godlike
wisdom. In other words, they weren't content to play second fiddle.
They weren't satisfied with being the created; they wanted to be the
Creator. They went after God's title.

Before the fall, none of our God-implanted desires or appetites was
sinful or wrong. They were, however, under the perfection of His plan,
to be governed by the spirit and thus, indirectly, by Him. But when

Adam and Eve chose to disobey, they were stating, in essence, that they were no longer content to be under His government. They wanted the constraints lifted. Genesis 3:6 says they found the tree of the knowledge of good and evil "desirable" to make them wise. Zodhiates defines this word as "ungoverned" desires.[1]

As stated above, the problem wasn't Adam and Eve's desire for wisdom or knowledge; the problem was coming out from under God's lordship to find these things. *Adam and Eve were honoring and choosing the will of soul over spirit.* This role reversal was devastating.

THE ULTIMATE DEATH

God had told Adam that if he ate the forbidden fruit he would "surely die" (Genesis 2:17), and indeed, the result of Adam's arrogance was death. Not instantly, in the physical sense—although, compared to what life was like for him prior to his rebellion, he might as well have died. Death meant the loss of God's life and separation from Him. It meant no longer enjoying unrestricted fellowship with his Maker. And for every human being since, the fall has spelled disaster. In fact, it was there that our tomb was formed, carved out of the rock of Adam's rebellion. The stone has been in place ever since, locking us into our dark world of death, destruction, and disorientation.

First, our spirit lost the *zoé* life God originally breathed into us (that is, we underwent spiritual death). God's Breath, or Spirit, was no longer inherently within us. This death that now enveloped man caused him to take on an entirely new nature; Ephesians teaches that before we come to Christ we are *"by nature children of wrath"* (2:3). Adam no longer had the Lord's perfection imbedded in him because he'd corrupted it. In that void, a completely unintended nature came to us all.

The word for "nature" in the above verse, *phusis*, means "lineage" and comes from a root meaning "to germinate or sprout; to bring forth or produce something."[2] By using this term, God is telling us this nature is more than symbolic—it's literal. When Adam sinned, he literally inherited a new nature that could produce and propagate nothing but sin in every realm of his being—body, soul, and spirit.

While Adam's spirit lost dominance with the departure of God's breath inside him, his soul was exalted to a position never intended. He would now do "what was right in his own eyes" (Judges 21:25). *The human race would now be ruled by the soul, which was controlled by Lucifer's inherited nature: pride and arrogance.* Humanism was instantly born, proclaiming that people are their own god. Self suddenly became the center of our existence. Before the fall, Adam no doubt exemplified the perfection found in Jesus. He was a servant-ruler who, in complete unselfishness, considered the needs and well-being of others before his own.

Rebellion brought all that to a screeching halt. Suddenly, satisfying the soul's cravings became Adam's number one desire. This new life-force—rooted in *psuché* (soul)—took preeminence. Therefore, *psuché* is often the word translated as "life" in the New Testament. Why? Because in our fallen world, *psuché* has become the motivating impetus. Adam was no longer controlled by *zoé* life emanating from his spirit and God's. His goal became to preserve and please the *psuché*, where self-rule had sprung up.

When you look around, don't you find that's still the world's primary modus operandi? Attorney and author Andrew Peyton Thomas perfectly captures the spirit of the fallen human race in his description of the effect selfishness has had on the United States:

> If the source of America's social disintegration is to be pinpointed so that it might be remedied, honesty compels us not to neglect this issue [of selfishness].... Self-centeredness and its related vices—crime, illegitimacy, child neglect—are exploding in America because, after centuries of Western philosophy devoted to the purpose, Americans are glorifying extreme individualism beyond

healthy limits, and beyond anything ever experienced by another national culture.[3]

But the problem isn't just American, it's human.

We call it humanism, but the human race is all about "me-ism." It was inevitable that we'd coin the term *humanism* so we could justify exalting ourselves. Suddenly it became okay to live by the philosophy that says if it feels good or seems right for me, do it. We justify wars and killing just like the son of Adam and Eve did after committing the first murder. We justify slavery and oppression. Abortion is so justified in mainstream culture that it's no longer an issue of slaughtering innocent babies—now it's a matter of individual rights. It's *my* body, *my* right, and I can do what I want with it; the life inside my womb is an inconvenience to me.

That, my friend, is the power of exalted *psuché*.

God help us all.

WHO KNOWS BEST?

Along with life becoming about fulfilling the soul's desires, the fall also brought about an exchange of logic. Rather than having God's *logos*, Adam (and through him, us) got his own limited knowledge of good and evil. Foolishly, we thought we knew best.

In *How Life Imitates the World Series*, Dave Boswell tells a story about Earl Weaver, former manager of the Baltimore Orioles. Sports fans will enjoy how he handled star Reggie Jackson.

Weaver had a rule that no one could steal a base unless given the steal sign. This upset Jackson because he felt he knew pitchers and catchers well enough to judge who he could and could not steal off of. So one game he decided to steal without a sign. He got a good jump and easily beat the throw to second. As he shook the dirt off his uniform, Jackson smiled with delight, feeling he had vindicated his judgment to his manager.

Later Weaver took Jackson aside and explained why he hadn't given the steal sign. First, the next batter was Lee May, his second-best power hitter. When Jackson stole second, first base was left open, so the other team walked May intentionally, taking the bat out of his hands.

Second, the next batter hadn't been strong against that pitcher, so Weaver felt he had to send up a pinch hitter to try to drive in the men on base. That left Weaver without bench strength later in the game when he needed it.

> **THE CREATOR SAW THE WHOLE PARADE. HE KNEW THE ULTIMATE HARM INDEPENDENT WISDOM, KNOWLEDGE, AND POWER MIGHT HAVE ON A CREATED BEING PRONE TO SELFISHNESS.**

The problem was, Jackson saw only his relationship to the pitcher and catcher. Weaver was watching the whole game.[4]

In the same way, Adam had his eyes only on what he could see—the possibility of becoming like God. The Creator, meanwhile, saw the whole parade. He knew the ultimate harm independent wisdom, knowledge, and power might have on a created being prone to selfishness.

By refusing God's *logos*, we in turn lost ultimate truth—*alétheia*—to the point that we now deny it exists at all. Instead of gaining true knowledge of good and evil, we became obsessed with proving relativism—no standard, no truth, all is subjective. That slippery slope has led us to an unmoored insanity that calls evil good and good evil

(Isaiah 5:20). Paul, under the Spirit's inspiration, describes it this way:

> They exchanged the truth of God for a lie, and wor-
> shiped and served the creature rather than the Creator,
> who is blessed forever....
>
> And just as they did not see fit to acknowledge God any
> longer, God gave them over to a depraved mind, to do those
> things which are not proper, being filled with all unright-
> eousness, wickedness, greed, evil; full of envy, murder, strife,
> deceit, malice; they are gossips, slanderers, haters of God,
> insolent, arrogant, boastful, inventors of evil, disobedient to
> parents, without understanding, untrustworthy, unloving,
> unmerciful; and although they know the ordinance of God,
> that those who practice such things are worthy of death, they
> not only do the same, but also give hearty approval to those
> who practice them. (Romans 1:25, 28–32)

Horrid. Ugly. But a painfully precise description of the fallen human race.

By elevating his soul and declaring God's wisdom

BY EXALTING THE SOUL, WE MADE OURSELVES UNABLE TO COMPREHEND THE THINGS OF GOD.

dom irrelevant or, at best, secondary, Adam went from being a *pneu-matikos* (a spiritual man) to a *psuchikos* (a soulish or natural man). His knowledge became limited to the natural world around him, and he became unable to discern spiritually. Paul spells this out:

> A natural man [*psuchikos*] does not accept the things of
> the Spirit of God, for they are foolishness to him; and he
> cannot understand them, because they are spiritually
> appraised. (1 Corinthians 2:14)

Please don't miss the strength of these words. It's not simply that humans *won't* accept the things of the spirit; it's that now we *cannot!* By exalting the soul, we made ourselves unable to comprehend the things of God. They are "foolishness" to us. The word is *môria*— moronish.[5] A "veil" was formed, keeping us from understanding God and from being spiritually discerning (2 Corinthians 4:3–4). As intelligent as we declare ourselves in the fields of physics, biochemistry, mathematics—you name it—we still remain completely ignorant in the Lord's classroom, where truth is found.

Think again about how God created us, and this result makes sense. The spirit was made to relate to the spiritual realm, which is where God, the Author of all supreme knowledge, dwells. The soul was merely meant to relate to the natural world, where only earthly information exists. This wasn't supposed to be our primary source of learning. But when we declared the soul our teacher, we forfeited understanding in the higher realm and chose to remain in the remedial class.

James gives a crystal-clear contrast of devolved and divine wisdom:

> If you have bitter jealousy and selfish ambition in your heart, do not be arrogant and so lie against the truth. This wisdom is not that which comes down from above, but is earthly, natural, demonic. For where jealousy and selfish ambition exist, there is disorder and every evil thing. But the wisdom from above is first pure, then peaceable, gentle, reasonable, full of mercy and good fruits, unwavering, without hypocrisy. And the seed whose fruit is righteousness is sown in peace by those who make peace. (3:14–18)

James points to many elements our natural minds wouldn't necessarily associate with wisdom. Purity, peace, submission, et al., are heavenly characteristics, ingredients of the spirit. And that's exactly the point. Our minds are stuck in the mud—*literally!* The wisdom we chose to follow (in place of God's *logos*) is bound to this earth. James even says that because it's earthly and natural, it's demonic. This doesn't mean natural knowledge is demonic, but rather that when our only source of knowledge is from the natural realm, it will inevitably be influenced by demons.

SEEING THROUGH SMOKE

Man used to have God's *logos;* now he has *psuché* logic. Paul describes this state of being led by our natural, earthly minds as a case of our being veiled and blinded:

> Even if our gospel is *veiled,* it is *veiled* to those who are perishing, in whose case the god of this world has *blinded* the minds of the unbelieving so that they might not see the light of the gospel of the glory of Christ, who is the image of God. (2 Corinthians 4:3–4)

The word *veil* (*kaluptô* or, in another form, *kalupsis*) means "to cover up or hide something."[6] For example, the inside of a tree is *kalupsis*-ed (veiled) by bark. The inside of the body is *kalupsis*-ed by skin. Anytime you wrap something so that it can't be seen, you have *kalupsis.* Paul uses this word in the most literal sense; the soulish human now has a covering over his mind that prohibits him from understanding spiritual truth. A filter, if you will. With truth hidden from him, he cannot understand the gospel, the context of this verse, or spiritual matters in general; it's like trying to stare through a fog or see clearly through a smokescreen.

Man will now need something supernatural—"beyond natural"— to see spiritual truth. He will need an unveiling, an *apokalupsis* . . . a revelation. Isn't it interesting that to create the word for a revelation, the Greeks simply added the prefix *apo* to *kalupsis?* The literal definition of revelation is simply to unveil or uncover. We would never have needed revelation, the lifting of the veil off our souls, if the fall had not occurred. We'll later look much more at the need for, and the process of, revelation.

Have you ever tried witnessing to a nonbeliever and failed miserably? I remember my first experience with this. I'd spent hours with a guy I'll call Scott. He wasn't a close friend, but I'd known him for several years and knew his story fairly well. In sharing the gospel with him, I'd gone the personal route, testifying to how Jesus had changed my life; I'd attempted the logical route, explaining the eternal options we had; and I'd even gone the apologetics route, defending why Christians believe

> **MAN WILL NOW NEED SOMETHING SUPERNATURAL— "BEYOND NATURAL"—TO SEE SPIRITUAL TRUTH.**

what we do and how we have proof to verify our beliefs. I was certain he would jump at the chance to believe, especially since he'd seen the radical change God had brought in me.

But when I asked if he wanted to accept Jesus as Lord and Savior, Scott simply replied, "Nope."

I asked why, and he replied, with the same nonchalance, "I just don't see any reason why I should."

We continued talking for another half-hour or so, but it became clear to me that this was an epic showdown between spirit and soul, one replayed every time an unbeliever is faced with the truth of the gospel. His soul won.

Scott didn't say no because he wanted to reject God but because he couldn't hear—*truthfully* hear—the message of my words. Why?

The veil covering his mind made it impossible to do so without the Spirit's intervention.

This even happens with people who've grown up around the truth of the gospel their entire lives.

> Few people know it, but both sets of Ernest Hemingway's grandparents were committed evangelical Christians. In fact, his paternal grandparents were both graduates of Wheaton College and very close friends of D. L. Moody. His maternal grandfather was such a godly patriarchal figure that his grandchildren called him "Abba." Furthermore, one of Hemingway's uncles was a missionary to China. Yet Ernest Hemingway, after leaving his evangelical rearing in Oak Park, Illinois, became the worldwide emblem of the lost generation who said, "I live in a vacuum that is as lonely as a radio tube when the batteries are dead and there is no current to plug into"—and who took his own life.[7]

Again, Paul says that Satan, "the god of this world," blinds the minds of those who don't know God (2 Corinthians 4:4). The term for this blindness (*tuphloó*) means "darken[ed] or smoky," yet inherent also in it is the essence of pride. A slightly different form, *tuphoô*, actually means "to inflate with self-conceit; to be lifted up with pride."[8] It's a perfect representation of the scenario created at the fall. When Adam exalted his soul above everything else, he and all humankind became blinded by pride, unable to see clearly into the spiritual realm. (There is a solution to this veiling and blindness, but we're not quite ready to go there.)

How Strong Is Your Soul?

Second Corinthians 10:5 says, "We are destroying *speculations* and every lofty thing raised up against the knowledge of God, and we are taking every thought captive to the obedience of Christ." The King James Version uses the word "imaginations." The Greek term is *logismos*, and it's not hard to notice its association with the word *logos*. This is humankind's own reasoning and logic, our own philosophies; Paul was telling us these have been exalted or "raised up against" God's knowledge. "Lofty thing[s]" (*hupsôma*) is from the same root word for "most high" God—*hupsistos*. Our "lofty thing," our pride, was exalted above God. Taking the place of God as our Most High was our soul—*psuché*. The resultant problems are beyond comprehension.

Once again: that is not how our Creator intended things to be. What was originally a spirit-led man (*pneumatikos*) became a spiritually dead man, who was ruled by his own enthroned, perverted soul (*psuché*). He has become a natural man (*psuchikos*), far removed from the condition through which he was supposed to relate to God. He lost life in his spirit and truth in his soul. Ironic, isn't it? The very thing meant to be the servant of the spirit now controlled Adam's entire being and placed him in direct rebellion to the Lord. This is the first of a two-part problem: an exalted soul.

The second facet of our dilemma, explained in the next chapter, involves the fallen soul's newfound susceptibility to strongholds. And, as we'll soon discover, it's where we encounter—and hopefully overcome—some of life's more gripping issues.

CHAPTER 5

MIND OVER MATTER

If you want a lesson on the psyche, ask Mercedes, my ninety-pound boxer. Probably not the first place you'd think about going for psychological insight, but the mind games she's played on me makes me positive she's on to something.

Lately it seems she has one goal in life: to escape our house whenever the front door opens. She thinks it's hilarious entertainment worthy of seven or eight daily repetitions. Trust me, it's not fun or funny to be calling neighbors for the sixth time in a weekend to ask, once again, whether they've seen your canine sniffing around next door or chewing up newspapers.

Now, I've been an extremely good master to Mercedes. I feed her and make sure she has fresh water. I let her out to do her business and clean up after her. Sometimes I play with her, or at least watch her "play" with our two *much* smaller dogs (guess who wins?). I even let her crawl up in my lap when we're watching TV. (I'd rather have her on my lap than licking my face, which is what I get when my lap is off-limits.)

None of my dutiful caregiving, however, seems to matter to her. Whether her little game of runaway was birthed out of boredom, spite, or instinct, I don't know. What I do know is how intent she is on proving that *she* is in control. Sometimes I'll open the door to find her staring me straight in the eye as she sits at the end of our driveway: "C'mon, Sheets ... just *try* and catch me." It's my will against hers. And even if her greatest success so far has been staying out a couple of hours, in her mind she's a winner every time.

In reality, Mercedes is a house dog. If she had her way and one day ran away for good, it's doubtful she'd long survive, battling the elements and rummaging for food. While running off may be all fun and games to her, I know better. That's why, with Ceci's "encouragement," despite the dog's shenanigans, I always go after Mercedes. And, every time so far, I've brought her back home to safety.

As we saw before, Adam had a different result—his game of runaway ended disastrously. After enjoying what could've been an eternity of living in the garden's complete perfection, he and Eve caved to the enemy's temptation. From that moment on, their game of hide-and-seek with God was no fun; in fact, it was something shameful that left permanent marks. God cannot tolerate sin, so He had to expel them from Eden. The communion was broken. Perfection was tainted.

Creation fell. You were there, whether you know it or not. In Adam we all died (1 Corinthians 15:22). The fall didn't just affect one man's relationship with his Maker; it threw our entire makeup out of balance. In the last chapter we saw the overall consequences, which is Part One of the problem: an exalted soul. Here we'll look at Part Two: the soul's potential for strongholds.

In discussing what happened to our soul, it's important to examine in greater detail how God wired us. If delving into how the soul functions sounds less exciting than a root canal, let me assure you that most people find what we're about to discuss to be one of the most revelatory segments of what's in this book. It will be anything but a boring "Psych 101" lecture. I only took one psychology course in college. I was so confused when it was over that I needed counseling!

I Seem to Remember . . .

Our memories are amazing things. It's said that Seneca the Elder, a famous first-century Roman orator and rhetorician, could repeat long passages of speeches he'd heard only a single time years before. In fact, the guy was so good he'd impress his students by asking each of them to recite a line of poetry, and after two hundred students had done so, he'd stand up and reel off their lines verbatim—in reverse order![1]

Okay, so most of us can't so impress a crowd. But I'm told we all have the capacity for such remarkable memories whether or not we realize it. The memory serves as a storage bank, a filing cabinet of sorts, where past experiences and information are kept. In combining the soul's intellectual and emotional dimensions, it keeps track of what we see, hear, feel, experience, and so forth. Some contend that *everything* we've ever seen or experienced is stored there, even though we can't consciously recall it. It's where information is when we say it's on the tip of our tongue.

Part of our soul is referred to as the subconscious mind, which includes the memory but does much more than just store information. By far, the majority of our mind's activity takes place there. What's the difference between the conscious and subconscious mind? The conscious mind is what processes cognitive activity—in other words, we're aware of what it's working on. The subconscious mind, however, is what acts involuntarily of the conscious. (*Sub* means "below the surface.")[2] Even while we're asleep it's churning away. Researchers estimate that the overwhelming majority—perhaps as much as 85 to 90 percent—of what takes place in our brains happens in our subconscious. Most of the time we're being controlled, or at the very least influenced, by this aspect of the soul. That is crucial for us to understand as we examine the effect our soul has on our overall being.

Our subconscious mind never stops working. It doesn't get tired or even rest. In sleep, our conscious shuts down and our subconscious takes over ... *voila*, dreams. (This is also why God seems to speak more frequently and clearly in our dreams; without consciousness in the way, we can be more open to divine revelation.)

This tireless part of the brain has an amazing capacity to observe and process. It picks up every minute detail of what's happening around us, every moment—every sound, color, feeling, reaction, etc. In fact, it even takes in what we're unaware of, such as what our peripheral vision is capturing, or the audible sounds our ears detect but our conscious mind doesn't process. According to Hans Moravec, a researcher and professor at Carnegie Mellon's Robotics Institute, the brain has a processing capacity of *one hundred trillion* instructions per second.[3] It's the ultimate filing cabinet. Truly astounding, isn't it? Makes "in His image" take on even greater meaning.

WHAT'S HOUSED IN THE SUBCONSCIOUS (MEMORY) SHAPES EVERY FACET OF WHO YOU ARE.

Not long ago, it was common to hear how the human brain could out-compute any machine. Now, however, it seems our ability to create faster and more complex computers has significantly narrowed the margin. In fact, Moravec estimates that computers are likely to surpass the brain's capacities by the year 2030.[4] For fans of the *Matrix* trilogy, that's not the most comforting news.

SECOND NATURE TAKES ITS COURSE

The brain isn't storing incalculable data each second just because it's a packrat. God wasn't just in a complicated mood when He made the subconscious so incomprehensibly complex. It was designed to serve an invaluable purpose: What's housed in the subconscious (memory) shapes every facet of who you are. What's stored there determines much of your personality, forms your habits (both good and bad), controls your actions and reactions, and basically becomes your belief center. In other words, *the sum total of what's stored there works together to determine what you really believe.*

Heavy stuff, huh? Let's think about this from various angles. Ponder, specifically, that our ability to remember facts shapes who we are. Sir Arthur Conan Doyle put it this way:

> I consider that a man's brain originally is like a little empty attic, and you have to stock it with such furniture as you choose. A fool takes in all the lumber of every sort that he comes across, so that the knowledge which might be useful to him gets crowded out, or at best is jumbled up with a lot of other things, so that he has difficulty in laying his hands upon it. Now, the skillful workman is very careful indeed as to what he takes into his brain-attic. He will have nothing but the tools which may help him in doing his work, but of these he has a large assortment, and all in the most perfect order.... It is of the highest importance, therefore, not to have useless facts elbowing out the useful ones.[5]

The "useful" facts run the gamut of daily living. Remember learning how to tie your shoes? If you're like me, the first dozen-or-so attempts, you had to think about each step. Take this string over here ... loop it under ... make a little bunny ear on this side ... wrap it around.... Imagine if we still went through that process every time we tied our shoes—sandal companies would be making a fortune! God made us in such a way that after repetition our subconscious mind assumes control and does the job for us. Now we can tie our shoes in our sleep—literally.

Typing is the same way. Most of us don't have to think through each letter and word, pecking it out at a snail's pace. As we learn the keyboard's arrangement and practice a bit, it increasingly becomes second nature. Soon we can watch news updates or handle phone calls while we type away.

There are thousands of examples: writing, swinging a bat, brushing our teeth, and so on. How about learning to drive—maddening, wasn't it? (especially if you started on a standard transmission). It seemed like you had to remember five hundred things at once: Keep right foot here. Push down with left foot and then let up, but not too much! Use right hand for gearshift, keep left hand on wheel. How many places to look when changing lanes? Oops, blinker. *Not* left foot on brake! . . .

Most of us were wrecks waiting to happen. But gradually it wasn't a big deal anymore. Our subconscious got it all stored and organized and took over; after a while the car became simply an extension of us, our subconscious capacities kicked in, and we went on cruise control.

BUILD-A-BELIEF . . . AND A STRONGHOLD

The subconscious mind does this with facts, processes, and techniques, but it also does the same with perceptions, feelings, thoughts, initial senses, and reactions. We build up information, or what we might call "mental images," and process them to the point of establishing *beliefs*. These are broad, underlying perceptions of how *we* think things really are. Doesn't mean they're true—they're merely our own version of reality. And as we store up all these images, we develop *belief systems*, often referred to as paradigms.

A paradigm is simply a mindset or a mind belief, *a grid of thought that serves as a filter for all our actions*. We have paradigms for business, race, spirituality, marriage, love, God . . . virtually everything. These develop according to what's been put in our memory bank.

Two factors determine (A) whether what's stored in the subconscious becomes a belief (controlling memory) and (B) its strength.

(1) Repetitious Information   This refers to how often we hear a certain fact, perform a certain action, or experience a certain emotion. For example, children who repeatedly experience affirming love and are embraced will begin to believe they have worth and act accordingly; children who repeatedly hear they're no good or are abused and rejected will begin to believe they're worthless and act accordingly. *The significance of repetitious information: how often we encounter it.*

(2) Impactful Information   Some things need only to be experienced once, or just a few times, for them to become indelibly imprinted on our soul. For example, the trauma of rape or the loss of a parent need not be repeated for the memory to become controlling. *The significance of impactful information: how we feel when we experience it.* A belief's strength is determined by a combination of repetition and intensity.

A BELIEF'S STRENGTH IS DETERMINED BY A COMBINATION OF REPETITION AND INTENSITY.

When the images stored in our memory banks are strong enough and negative in nature (destructive, painful, and so forth), a massive structure of negative belief is erected. The Bible calls this a *stronghold*, the second facet of the problem we're discussing. Paul uses this word in talking about what we war against in our mind (2 Corinthians 10:4). The Greek term *ochurôma* means "a castle, fortress, stronghold;

a place from which to rule or hold onto something."⁶ The root word *echô* means "to have or hold."⁷

Generically, a stronghold can serve a productive purpose, but in Scripture the word is used in a negative sense. Strongholds are, biblically speaking, inappropriate fortresses constructed in our mind from which we can be ruled or controlled. They're beliefs—conscious and subconscious—through which we're so held captive that we can't escape on our own. In fact, *ochurôma* was also used as the word for a prison. For those bound by a stronghold, make no mistake about it—that's exactly what these areas of the soul become.

> **STRONGHOLDS ARE, BIBLICALLY SPEAKING, INAPPROPRIATE FORTRESSES CONSTRUCTED IN OUR MIND FROM WHICH WE CAN BE RULED OR CONTROLLED.**

Once, walking through the twisted little streets of Kowloon in Hong Kong, I came upon a tattoo studio. In the window were displayed samples of the tattoos available. On the chest and arms you could have tattooed an anchor or flag or mermaid or whatever. But what struck me with force were three words that could be tattooed on one's flesh, *Born to lose.* I entered the shop in astonishment and, pointing to those words, asked the artist, "Does anyone really have that terrible phrase tattooed on his body?" He replied, "Yes, sometimes." "But," I said, "I just can't believe that anyone in his right mind would do that." The Chinese man simply tapped his forehead and said, in broken English, "Before tattoo on body, tattoo on mind."⁸

Strongholds are negative, destructive thought patterns tattooed on the mind. If allowed to develop, they can imprison a person for life.

Before the fall, Adam and Eve had no strongholds. Everything in their minds was wholesome, life-producing, security-building, love-motivated. There were no cloying fears, painful memories, unclean habits, or wrong beliefs to deal with. *Since the fall, the mind has become susceptible to strongholds of every kind.*

DISTORTING REALITY

Satan doesn't have to be directly involved in the forming of a stronghold. Our mind can do this very well on its own. But Satan and his demons are master designers when it comes to strongholds. They're the premier architects, builders, contractors, and realtors all in one. As the father of lies, Satan's method is to use—you guessed it—deception. He takes the thoughts and feelings we receive into our subconscious, infuses the information with his interpretation, and skillfully forms them into belief systems.

One of the things that often makes his tactics so effective is that he uses real events and factual impressions. You really were rejected by your father when he left your family. Your husband really did cheat on you. You actually were called ugly as a teenager. He then reminds us again and again of these occurrences and distorts them with his interpretations to the point that we accept his suggestions as truth. They then become a part of our belief system. In this way, something that occurred years, maybe decades, ago can control us.

In keeping with how the soul works, this leads to another important point: *What happens to us (the facts) is not really what creates a stronghold; what we believe about what happens to us is what creates a stronghold.* That's pretty heavy. Events in and of themselves are either pleasant or unpleasant, but our belief about them determines whether they are constructive or destructive. Occurrences are either good or bad—there's nothing we can do to change that; but we decide through what we believe about them whether they're beneficial or detrimental.

Put another way, when it comes to destructive events, our present struggles have more to do with defensive images and beliefs that we hold now than with the victimization of the past. We've convinced ourselves that the images—resulting beliefs—held in our subconscious are in fact truth, even if they're contrary to the glimpses of real truth we catch every now and then in God's mirror, His Word. And the human will to survive, no matter what that survival looks like, is a staggering force.

So we develop ways to coexist with untruths that have become our reality. We form coping mechanisms that help us make life work or minimize the pain we feel. For example, we build relational walls to protect us from getting abused or rejected again. We discover how to fake intimacy with people so that we don't really have to get close to them and risk being hurt all over again. And when we use coping mechanisms like these, we're simply reinforcing the stronghold, adding another brick to Satan's fortress inside us. All of us have faced these crafty schemes of the enemy. Obviously, this is not how God intended it to be.

You Don't Easily Forget a Stronghold

It's no small thing to deal with strongholds. They are a very serious issue. When they're strong enough, they can cause people to turn psychotic. One day a father is living what seems to be a normal life with his wife and two kids, the next day he's shot them all in his own home and turned the gun on himself. Why? Because he was abused by his dad as a little boy and, buying into the beliefs of fear and inadequacy, was convinced he was a failure as a husband and father. Strongholds of the soul are what drive mass-murderers, rapists, child molesters, wife beaters, etc. Sure, demonic forces are at work in those situations, but they operate through strongholds of the soul. Most of the fortresses you and I deal with are not as severe, but nonetheless can be just as controlling.

For instance, when I was in the fourth grade I was thrown in with the youth group at my church for a Scripture memorizing ordeal. We were supposed to memorize a few verses and then go in front of the whole congregation and recite them. For some reason, when it was my turn, I completely froze. I couldn't remember those Scriptures for the life of me.

Normally when something like that happens, the leader is kind enough to help prompt you along. Not for me. Rather than cover up for me or offer some clues, the person actually started ridiculing and making fun of me in front of everyone. It was absolutely humiliating. As I stood there I began to cry, which then embarrassed me even more. And believe it or not, the leader actually got mad at me for crying in front of everyone and told me to go sit down.

It was a horrible experience that left such a mark on me that until my sophomore year in college I couldn't stand up in front of people and talk. I'm not exaggerating when I say, I'd get my name out (barely) and my brain would suddenly shut down. Everything in my head would revert back to my fourth-grade experience, and my mind would go blank. Talk about a stronghold!

This experience consumed and bound me. It didn't make any difference what I consciously tried to do to change my image or belief; whenever I faced a public speaking situation, my subconscious triggered the same reaction. It believed wholeheartedly that I would never be able to speak in front of people. Looking back, perhaps an evil spirit was at work that day, knowing the call of God on my life. Granted, our enemy doesn't know everything. But I believe that through observation he's well aware of what God is doing in a person's life and pounces on any opportunity to destroy or ruin that progression. Even at that young age—no, *especially* at that young age—the enemy of my soul was trying to thwart what God desired for me. It wasn't until I was twenty-one years old that the stone was rolled away for me. That's how subtle yet powerful Satan can be in erecting strongholds in our life.

BANKING IN THE BRAIN

My experience shows how fundamental the subconscious mind is in forming and shaping our beliefs. And it brings us to another critical point for understanding strongholds: They produce *involuntary* actions. What is believed in our subconscious mind is what we will ultimately act out (1) *whether or not we want to*; (2) *whether or not we realize* it's why we're acting a certain way; and (3) *even if we're not consciously aware* that the stronghold exists. Bummer!

I didn't realize until much later in life why I was so petrified of speaking in public. I can't count the number of times I've heard people lament the fact that they don't know why they do the things they do. The answer lies hidden in the subconscious.

Earlier I used the term *memory bank*, and indeed, that's what the subconscious mind is. Just like a real bank, it has various currencies it deals with. Some images it processes come in the form of $1 bills; what you think an ideal family should look like, for example, may be in this category. Other images can be slotted as $5 bills; those may be your beliefs on what it means to be a Christian. Others serve as your mind's $10 bills, $20 bills, and on up. But all of these currencies together comprise a storehouse of denominations—a bank, if you will. The sum total of these denominations or images is your belief center. Ultimately, whatever is in there is what you can and will spend.

While not always a pleasant thing to accept, especially when we're frustrated in trying to change certain character traits, nevertheless this is the truth. But once we understand that the subconscious deals with the overwhelming majority of the brain's activity, and does so without our consciously being aware of it, it makes sense that our subconscious has the real say-so in what we believe and how we act. We may even consciously choose to believe something else, but until it is accepted and believed in our subconscious, our belief center, we will not permanently change.

If for most of your life you've struggled with a negative self-image, then you've no doubt discovered by now that consciously choosing to believe something contrary to what's in your subconscious doesn't

> **CONSCIOUSLY CHOOSING TO BELIEVE SOMETHING CONTRARY TO WHAT'S IN YOUR SUBCONSCIOUS DOESN'T BRING LASTING DIFFERENCE.**

bring lasting difference. Maybe you have anger issues and have repeatedly determined that you will no longer yield to the rage. But when you find yourself in a situation that touches that hidden place inside you, something seemingly uncontrollable and probably not understood starts to rise up from deep within. This will always be the case until what's in the subconscious—the storage bank, your belief center—is changed.

I've counseled countless people who go through this. Eventually they found that while it was wonderful when their conscious mind accepted a new paradigm of truth, their subconscious mind still had to receive it—otherwise, deep within their belief center they were still controlled by a stronghold. The subconscious is *not* changed simply by a conscious choice.

I had a friend who was a pastor in New York.[9] For the first three years of his marriage, his wife had no sexual relationship with him. Because she'd been raped as a twelve-year-old girl, she couldn't bring herself to engage in intercourse. No matter how much she tried to overcome her trauma and the fear that continued to haunt her, she just couldn't.

It wasn't that she was naïve about the situation or too stubborn to seek help. She'd received counseling. She'd tried consciously choosing to believe the truth about herself, her husband, and the pleasure God intended for a husband and wife through the intimacy of intercourse. And, as a pastor's wife, she'd heard countless sermons about God's ability to free her. But ultimately none of this made a difference because she hadn't successfully changed the negative content that resided in her subconscious mind and shaped her beliefs. When she found herself in similar enough circumstances to the original trauma, the subconscious—the memory—sent the information to the surface, and her past began to control her present.

THE CIRCLE OF SOUL-LIFE

We often hear the term *willpower* in discussing how to overcome a stronghold. I've heard it said, "Set your will and you can do this." Yes, the will causes us to act, but it does so based on what's in the mind and emotions.

The will is directly controlled by these two other parts of the soul. Its hands are tied by what the mind and emotions pass on to it. Stated another way, *the entrance to the will is through the mind and emotions* (which, as we've already learned, include the subconscious/memory).

We have to go through the mind and emotions—including this storage bank of memories—to get to the will and turn something into action. Wouldn't it be easier if we could simply make a decision from our spirit, bypass what's in the soul, and just be like Jesus all the time? Unfortunately, that's not possible. Let me reinforce what I've been saying by illustrating exactly how this entire process of the soul works.

When an event, word, sound, feeling, etc., enters your soul—your spouse makes a statement, you see a billboard, you perceive a certain

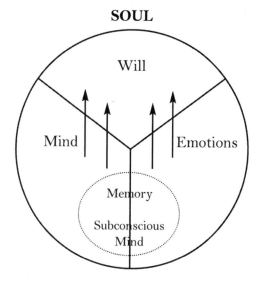

scent—whatever occurs, *it first goes to your subconscious mind,* not the conscious. (This is why subliminal advertising works so well. Marketers have learned how to concentrate on the part of your brain that *really* makes the decisions.)

So the outside stimulus is first received into your subconscious, which has filed *every single detail* of past occurrences (remember how incredibly acute the memory bank is). Like a Google search, within a nanosecond it searches massive archives for anything that even remotely connects to this new information. Perhaps a smell triggers childhood recollections of your grandma's kitchen. A color scheme reminds you of last summer's beachfront vacation spot. Or on the negative side, a disagreement in a meaningful relationship evokes memories of the friend or parent who walked out. *An opinion or impression is formed before you even have time to consciously think about it.*

I remember meeting a guy who had just returned from Vietnam. He suffered from post-traumatic stress disorder. In his case, any loud noise triggered an involuntary reaction. I saw this firsthand one evening while in his apartment. We were thick into conversation when someone in the outside hallway slammed their door. Before I knew what was happening, he jumped out of his seat, leaped over the couch, and was crouched in a shooting position. All before he'd even had time to think about it!

He was terrified, and then embarrassed. When things settled down, I learned that he'd reacted this way out of necessity during the war when coming under fire. His brain had processed those events in such a way that any sound reminiscent of gunshots *automatically* triggered a similar response.

The same kind of reflex can occur with those who've been abused. I once stood next to a boy who'd apparently been beaten so often that when I made a sudden movement with my arm, he instantly flinched and covered his face. It was heartbreaking.

In each case, the person's subconscious took a bit of information that seemed reminiscent of a pattern of pain or trauma and made an instant association. Instantly it pulled the file of the haunting memory, and the result was a repeated involuntary reaction. Neither reasoning nor logic will change this system when dealing with a stronghold. My pastor friend's wife, for instance, was extremely levelheaded about her condition. She reasoned with herself, telling herself that her fear shouldn't control her to the point of frigidity. She made a conscious decision, and her reason and intellect *were* confirming her fervent appeal for freedom. I had done the same with my fear of speaking. Frustratingly, at that stage, it was to no avail for either of us.

Whether the deduction or impression made in your subconscious evokes memories of pain or pleasure, the final step in this process involves passing that information on to the conscious mind. This is where we can think about it and analyze it. But recall that before we do, we already have our opinion formed. *This is also why it's so hard for*

MIND AND EMOTIONS

Stimulus

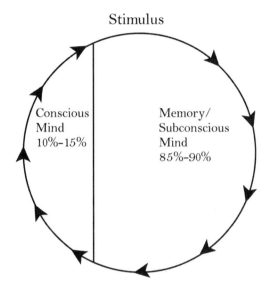

us to accept new truth. When we hear it, we already have a subconscious opinion before we are able to consciously think about it.

IT'S ALL ABOUT PERCEPTION

We've already noted that it's possible to believe something regardless of whether or not it's true. Our intellect and emotions process current events according to what we believe, regardless of the beliefs' validity. And this brings us to a sobering thought. We've danced around it, but now I want to clearly state this unavoidable point: What we believe to be true in our subconscious controls us and shapes who we are whether it is true or not. *We are not controlled by truth—we are controlled by what we believe to be truth.* Scary, but true.

Proverbs 23:7 says, "As [a man] hath thought in his soul, so [is] he" (YLT). Most translations use the word *heart* instead of *soul*, but the Hebrew term, *nephesh*, does in fact mean "soul." It's referring to exactly the part of us we've been talking about. As you think in your soul—your conscious *and* subconscious mind—so are you. Plato once said, "Thinking is the talking of the soul with itself."[10] That soul-talk ultimately creates your version of truth, regardless of how factual it is (or isn't).

WE ARE NOT CONTROLLED BY TRUTH—WE ARE CONTROLLED BY WHAT WE BELIEVE TO BE TRUTH.

There's more depth to this verse in Proverbs, however. Another Hebrew word, *shaar,* is translated as "hath thought," but its literal meaning displays just how insightful the writer was regarding the soul's operation. *Shaar* means "to split or open;"[11] used for a doorkeeper or gatekeeper, it refers to a place of access or an entranceway. In this context, *shaar* isn't pointing to what's consciously thought but to what's given access to the soul—to what causes the thinking. Notice the difference? Whatever a person opens the gate of his soul to, *that's* what causes his thinking. That, in turn, creates the person's reality.

This isn't necessarily a voluntary act. The pastor's wife had no control over her childhood circumstances, and she didn't have control over how her subconscious would process the trauma and file it away. Yet as her soul's gates were forced open, her subconscious kicked in and began creating a truth that said all men—even her husband, years later—would eventually violate or hurt her. Her will responded by shutting down her body at even the hint of intercourse.

Snakes, Sweat Drops, and Blisters

Psychological research has repeatedly proven the power of the mind's perception in creating reality. An article in *Reader's Digest* said,

Gut feelings can occur without a person being consciously aware of them. For example, when people who fear snakes are shown a picture of a snake, sensors on their skin will detect sweat, a sign of anxiety, even though the people say they do not feel fear. The sweat shows up even when a picture is presented so rapidly that the subject has no conscious awareness of seeing it.[12]

The subconscious picked up on the image and was already programmed to respond with a measurable response of fear.

Another example is found in the field of hypnosis.* It's been proven that, under hypnosis, a person's subconscious beliefs clearly trump the reality of a situation. One hypnotist told his subject to hold out her hand, then announced that he was going to put a hot coal in it, but instead he placed an ice cube there. Despite reality, she immediately dropped the ice cube . . . and a blister formed on her hand.[13]

How can this be? *The subconscious mind believed the hypnotist's words.* It pulled the file that associated holding a hot coal with pain and, working on autopilot, sent impulses throughout the body that caused a blister. *What's believed in the subconscious doesn't have to be true to control us; it merely has to be believed.*

A Mighty Fortress Is Our Subconscious

Getting the picture? The subconscious is a powerful force to be reckoned with. It does not deal lightly with the events of our lives, but like a court reporter is feverishly taking notes of every detail that passes through our senses. From the sum total of these words and events, we create fixed representations of what we *believe* things to be.

*I do not believe a Christian should be hypnotized. Hypnosis, which gives another person access straight to the subconscious, bypasses the conscious mind and allows the hypnotist to plant into the subconscious whatever seeds he or she desires. Depending on the person involved, this could result in demonic forces being invited into the soul.

And from these beliefs—true or false, good or bad—we are controlled.

It should be obvious by now that these soul-shaping experiences aren't limited to things others have done to us. As we recognize our soul's weak spots, we'll discover that sometimes they're caused by "minor" situations we've brought upon ourselves and allowed to fester too long. A "slight" problem with envy that was never truly uprooted. A "tiny" habit of cheating that we never faced head on. A "little bit" of laziness that never got straightened out. But don't forget: The enemy of our soul will take any ground he's granted. And territory gained inch by inch over years becomes a matter of miles.

It's time we tear down the strongholds we've created ourselves, had forced upon us, or allowed Satan to build. How do we carry this out? How do we keep future strongholds from being built? How can we really start anew within our subconscious, especially if it's not a matter of just telling our conscious mind to "get better"? These are questions we will continue to answer with various strategies throughout this book.

For now, remember this: Before the fall, every facet of Adam and Eve's soul was controlled by the Holy Spirit. They were governed by His knowledge and His presence. Everything was in perfect balance, in perfect order. They didn't struggle with strongholds or listen to enemy lies. They were one with God, walking in complete union with their Maker.

That's not just a pep talk to get us yearning for the days of Eden. As we'll see, it's a reality that God has every intention of restoring, if we'll allow Him.

PART II

THE PROVISION

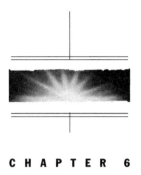

CHAPTER 6

BACK TO LIFE

I was in a play. Once. For all of two minutes.

And after my performance, I decided to do the smart thing: I retired from my acting career while I was on top.

Okay, so I was in the fifth grade. But still, after playing my role that evening, in front of a packed house of at least a thousand ... all right, maybe it was more like a crowd of eight hundr—... yeah, eighteen parents showed up on a rainy Wednesday night. But I'm sure at least *twice* that many kids were there, even if they *were* forced to go with their parents.

Anyway, I played a mean PRINCE #3; he was the good guy, the hero of the entire play. The story was about a rich princess who'd been promised by a wizard that one day she'd meet her Prince Charming. To protect her from suitors only after her money, the wizard cast a spell that made her unable to smile until the day she encountered her one true love.

She waited and waited until a prince showed up claiming he was the one. He wasn't. But he somehow tricked the princess's parents into believing that she could now smile, and as soon as they handed over her fortune, he rode off into the sunset with her. Lo and behold, a second prince appeared on the scene, promising the king and queen he'd rescue their daughter from the fake prince—only he too was a con artist. He'd arranged with the other prince to stage a rescue in hopes of scamming a royal reward.

After a little more trickery, with the damsel in dire distress, finally a true prince—that's me!—came riding out of the woods with beaming princess in tow. How did everyone know this was the real deal? Allow me to recite my infamous (and only) lines, which I eloquently delivered to the king and queen:

> PRINCE #3: Your majesties, though I am
> honored by your offer, I wish not a sin-
> gle share of your fame and fortune as
> reward. For I have already found my
> treasure, and it is in your daughter's
> smile.
>
> [MOTION TO PRINCESS, DRAMATIC PAUSE]
>
> May our love be as true as her radiant
> countenance.

The crowd went wild (even though I stumbled over "countenance"). The curtains came down. A thunderous standing ovation continued, and surely tears poured freely from every man, woman, and child present. Though I'd appeared onstage for only a moment, it was clear to me who they were applauding. I'd certainly go down in Keller Elementary history as the greatest scene-stealing thespian ever.

Anyway, that's how my mom tells the story. At any rate, my overcoming of wicked imposters was no doubt prophetic of my calling!

REAL-LIFE DRAMA

To start his gospel, John writes about the ultimate scene-stealer, profoundly setting the stage for the drama of all dramas:

In the beginning was the Word, and the Word was with God, and the Word was God. He was in the beginning with God. All things came into being through Him, and apart from Him nothing came into being that has come into being. In Him was life, and the life was the Light of men. The Light shines in the darkness, and the darkness did not comprehend it. . . .

He was in the world, and the world was made through Him, and the world did not know Him. He came to His own, and those who were His own did not receive Him. (1:1–5, 10–11)

Within eighteen verses, John paints a perfect picture of the world's history. Act One describes its foundations and reveals the role of Jesus in creating it. Act Two tells of the fall, how the creation no longer knew its Creator.

In showing Christ as having "life," life that "was the Light of men," John's point isn't only to emphasize that Jesus created life. The verse doesn't say, "In Him was *bios*," the Greek word for physical life; it's a given that Jesus created the world. No, this gloriously simple description of Jesus' purpose in coming to earth puts the spotlight on one factor: *zoé*. In Him was *zoé*. *God's* life. Something people had been missing for a long time.

Jesus had come to restore *abundant life* (John 10:10). Divine life. The spiritual death that had buried us could be broken. It's as if John were screaming, "Look! There's finally a human being on the planet that has *zoé* again! There's hope! Four thousand years of spiritual death and the life of God is once more in man!"

Indeed, hope *was* restored through the one God-man. Within the context of the fall, we recognize Jesus as the ultimate Redeemer. Unless we see restoration in the context of what we lost (in Genesis), we misunderstand and fail to comprehend the significance of what

Jesus said and did. It loses its relevance. As the second and last Adam (1 Corinthians 15:45), Christ came to restore *zoé* to all humanity. That He was called "the last Adam" is important; it indicates that He represented the entire race, just as the first Adam did. Through Adam, we lost *zoé*, God's life in us, and, alienated from Him, instead functioned out of *psuché*, with its fallen life-force. We had physical life—*bios*—but Jesus brought the possibility of receiving God's life again. For the first time in thousands of years, *zoé* once again walked among us. Now, *that's* a way to steal a scene.

And, in Jesus' case, the thunderous applause will never end.

UNDERSTANDING REINTRODUCED

So far we've spent five chapters dealing with the problem humanity faced after Adam's rebellion. We've described why we fell, what that fall meant to our makeup, and how our fallen nature affects us all today through our exalted soul and the existence of strongholds. In the process, we've learned specifically what we lost: God's *zoé* (life), *Pneuma* (Spirit), *logos* (understanding/wisdom/logic), and *alétheia* (truth).

With Jesus' arrival on earth, each of those four elements was reintroduced. Jesus came to make possible the restoration of God's life to us. Jesus also restored God's breath to us through the Holy Spirit (John 20:22). God's *Pneuma* was restored within us through Jesus.

JESUS IS THE WORD (*LOGOS*); GOD'S MESSAGE TO US, GOD'S LOGIC.

Along with these was another crucial element Jesus came to restore: God's "Word." Not the entire Bible—that wouldn't be fully revealed just yet. John wasn't referring only to the words Christ would say, either. Jesus *is* the Word (*Logos*; John 1:1); God's message to us, God's logic. Jesus brought understanding of the divine.

Through Him we could once again receive the ability to think His thoughts, hear His voice, understand His ways, receive His revelation.

Jesus didn't merely preach God's message, He embodied it. Granted, He gave us *rhémas*, "spoken words,"[1] and He inspired the *graphé* (the Scriptures). But more fundamental to our redemption, Jesus is the *Logos*. We had trampled on God's knowledge by exalting our own. Yet, in His love, God sent a living human being, His Son, who embodied every facet of Himself. By understanding Jesus, we could regain our understanding of God. He would begin the process through His life on earth and continue it by restoring our ability to hear God's voice.

John 1:18 reveals this beautiful truth: "No one has seen God at any time; the only begotten God who is in the bosom of the Father, He has explained Him." In other words, we'd lost our ability to see and understand God. Recall that God walked with Adam in the garden—that's the kind of relationship we were intended to have. But after the fall, we became blinded by our pride and could no longer see our Maker. Even Socrates, in soulish wisdom, recognized our need when he said, "Oh, that someone would arise, man or god, to show us God."[2]

Whether a renowned philosopher or, as in the following story, a small child, we're all looking for God.

> Soon after her brother was born, little Sachi began to ask her parents to leave her alone with the new baby. They worried that like most four-year-olds, she might feel jealous and want to hit or shake him, so they said no. But she showed no signs of jealousy. She treated the baby with kindness, and her pleas to be left alone with him became more urgent. They decided to allow it.
>
> Elated, she went into the baby's room and shut the door, but it opened a crack—enough for her curious

parents to peek in and listen. They saw little Sachi walk up to her baby brother, put her face close to his, and say quietly, "Baby, tell me what God looks like. I'm starting to forget."[3]

Jesus came to re-declare God to us so we could once again see Him. As John says, He came to "explain" Him to us. The Greek term is *exegeomai*;[4] it's where we get our word *exegete*, which means to explain something by dissecting it for a more detailed look. To exegete a verse is to take it apart, word by word, to get an amplified meaning of each part; you then bring those expanded pieces back together to see with increased clarity the meaning contained within the entire verse. Jesus exegeted God, "breaking Him down" so that we, despite our soul-veiled minds, could once again understand Him.

The meaning of this is profound: No longer was God an ambiguous presence as He'd been to so many throughout the Old Testament period. Now if we wanted to know how God thinks, we could look at Jesus. What makes Him angry? Look at Jesus. Is He moved to compassion, and what makes Him laugh? Look at Jesus. *Everything* about God was explained through Christ. Dr. Donald Grey Barnhouse points this out through the words of Nicodemus: "Thou art a teacher come from God." Not only that, says Barnhouse: "Jesus was more— He was God come to teach!"[5]

IGNORING THE TRUTH

Jesus came to restore God's life, Spirit, and word. Finally, He also entered our *psuché*-dominated realm as the bearer of absolute truth. Without Him, we were destined for deception, thanks to our sin of trying to enthrone ourselves in God's place. As Jack Nicholson memorably said in *A Few Good Men*, we could no longer handle the truth. Instead we put on a continual charade, pretending everything was fine.

Former NBA center and coach Johnny Kerr said his biggest coaching test came when he led the then-expansion team Chicago Bulls; his tallest player was 6' 8" Erwin Mueller.

"We'd lost seven in a row, and I decided to give a psychological pep talk before a game with the Celtics," Kerr said. "I told Bob Boozer to go out and pretend he was the best scorer in basketball. I told Jerry Sloan to pretend he was the best defensive guard. I told Guy Rogers to pretend he could run an offense better than any other point guard, and I told Erwin Mueller to pretend he was the best rebounding, shot-blocking, scoring center in the game.

"We lost the game by seventeen. I was pacing around the locker room afterward trying to figure out what to say when Mueller walked up, put his arm around me, and said, 'Don't worry about it, coach. Just pretend we won.'"[6]

Unfortunately, we also have been trying to pretend we've won the game ever since we left the garden—and not the Boston Garden. We've acted as if our souls are without need of redemption. We've excused our sin, downplayed it, even denied it, but none of our self-defense or redirection changes the reality that without the intervention of a Savior representing the absolute truth, we are doomed.

In John 14:6, Jesus declares Himself to be "the way, and the truth, and the life; no one comes to the Father but through Me." All who reject Christ's message hate these words. Through them, Jesus made clear His claims, drawing the line in the sand for all who want to find God. The three main terms used in Jesus' statement are *hodos* ("the way"), *alétheia* ("truth"), and *zoé* ("life"). The latter two we've already defined; *hodos*, "a path or road that leads to something," is the root from which we get the word *method*. Jesus is the method, the road that leads to ... what? Truth and life. He is the way back to *truth for our soul* and *life for our spirit*. He is the means to our restoration, our recovery. While our exalted soul may defend itself by arguing that truth is nonexistent or, at best, defined by us, God says otherwise— and, as the Creator of all life, He gets the last call.

> **JESUS IS THE METHOD, THE ROAD THAT LEADS TO TRUTH AND LIFE. HE IS THE WAY BACK TO TRUTH FOR OUR SOUL AND LIFE FOR OUR SPIRIT.**

INTEGRATING SALVATION

Now, in our quest for the rediscovery of what we lost, we come to a major question: How does that which Christ came to restore actually make its way into our lives? Yes, we confess we're sinners, put our faith in His sacrifice, and get saved. But then we must proffer a foundational query, one that, sadly, most Christians can't accurately answer. What does it really mean to be "saved"?

Obviously, most believers accept God's truth that we are in need of the Savior; that's the fundamental admittance leading to our salvation. We wouldn't be Christians without confessing that we have a sin/soul problem and that we need redemption to be saved. But while most of us know this, we misunderstand just what being "saved" really means.

Huh? C'mon, Sheets. It's simple: You accept Jesus as Savior and it's over. Your soul gets saved and instantly transformed. God takes the old you and suddenly makes it new again so you have eternal access into His kingdom.

Yes and no. There's actually a BIG difference in how your spirit and soul are saved. Humongous. Astronomical. Gi-normous. And here's where we begin to understand *"If I am, why don't I?"* Countless disillusioned, I-tried-Jesus-but-He-didn't-work-for-me people have been devastated because no one explained to them that God's provision for us—our salvation—affects our spirit and soul differently. *Our spirit is changed instantly; our soul is not.* Our spirit is made brand-new at salvation; our soul is not. Our spirit looks like Jesus; our soul does not. (Remember, the soul is the mind, emotions, and will.)

Perhaps not comprehending this has left you frustrated more than a time or two. Recall those contradictions we dis-

> **OUR SPIRIT IS CHANGED INSTANTLY; OUR SOUL IS NOT.**

cussed—the Bible says as believers we're a certain way, while our daily life says otherwise. What doesn't occur in the soul at conversion is the reason why.

In the next few chapters we'll examine what takes place in our spirit at conversion, versus what occurs in our soul. We will look at the cross through a different lens and gain new perspective on this amazing act of love and sacrifice. Much from Christ's life will finally make sense, including some of His most important words.

We'll also examine how our lack of true understanding has distorted the message of salvation, making it anemic and misleading. Some of what I share is strong and hard-hitting, but I assure you it's neither to jump on a hobbyhorse nor to beat you up in any way. It's simply to say that "the greatest story ever told" is not being told with enough clarity, and that the greatest need of our lives—God's salvation—is not being clearly understood.

The results, as you'll see, have been catastrophic. The stone remains in place for many—out of their sarcophagus but stuck in the grave chamber, the door to real life remaining locked. We live schizophrenic Christian lives, and much of God's provision for us is wasted. He's misunderstood, Christianity gets a black eye, and unnecessary pain and suffering continue. This cycle must stop! It can. And we're going to do our part.

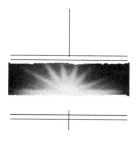

CHAPTER 7

THE BEING AND THE BECOMING

I don't remember being born. Not many of us do, though I've known a couple of individuals who recall vague notions of their experience. Personally, I'm thankful my mind—my *conscious* mind, that is—doesn't haunt me with memories of being squeezed out a tiny passageway, landing in cold, rubber-gloved hands, having fingers shoved down my throat, or being turned upside-down and my backside slapped. (Anyway, I have a hard enough time remembering where I left my keys!)

But I certainly will never forget being born again. It was as if I'd been living life in black and white only to awaken to a vibrant, hi-def world. Personalities shone brighter and more beautifully. Words took on new meaning. Sights triggered new senses. Dreams came saturated with profound messages. Accepting Christ seemed to change virtually every facet of my existence. And yet I could hardly explain what *really* happened. Instead of instant answers, I had an endless list of questions. How in the world could the God of the universe "come into my heart"? What was all this talk about being "washed and cleansed by the blood of Jesus"? And how was it even possible for me, at nineteen, to be "born again"?*

Apparently I wasn't alone. George Barna, master of statistics, has conducted several surveys involving those who've been "born again." The results prove that we believers having all gone through a similar spiritual experience doesn't mean we think the same.

- One-third of those born again say that a person can get to heaven by "being good enough."
- Twenty-eight percent of those born again believe that, while He was on earth, Jesus committed sins just like the rest of us.
- Sixty-four percent of born-again adults and 83 percent of born-again teenagers say moral truth is not absolute but circumstantial.

These statistics may not surprise you, but they should alarm you. You may know people who would agree with each of those groups (given the percentages, it's probable you do). But isn't it odd how being born again can put us all on the same page spiritually, yet many of us are leagues away when it comes to the soul's understanding of that experience? How else do we explain the variance of beliefs in such fundamental, biblical truths? Clearly, our *psuché* needs some realigning.

Before we get into the soul's transformation, though, let's look at what happens to our spirit when we're saved (or born again). This is important, because not only does it define what we receive into our spirit, it also reveals the potential for our soul. First Peter 1:23 says, "You have been born again not of seed which is perishable but imperishable, that is, through the living and enduring word of God." Only

---

*I was actually born again as a small child, but I walked away from God when I was seventeen. When I recommitted my life to Christ, the impact was so profound it felt like I was being born again for the first time.

two times does the New Testament contain the expression "born again": this verse and when Jesus spoke with Nicodemus (John 3). So seldom used, and yet such a fundamental part of Christianity that when we're "saved," most of us refer to it as being "born again." Why is this? Partially because that's *exactly* what happens through salvation.

You're a Tailor-Made Replica!

When Peter describes us as being "born again"—*anagennaô*—he's being completely literal. The moment we accept God's offer of *zoé* life through Jesus Christ, we are instantly reborn of God in our spirit. *Spiritually we receive the very life and nature of God Himself, just like it was before the fall. Anagennaô* can be broken down into two words: *gennaô*, meaning "to procreate, beget something, or regenerate"; and *ana*, "again."[1]

You can see the words *gene, genetic,* and *gender,* in *gennaô.* It truly is a reproductive term. We're not just "adopted" into God's family (Ephesians 1:5), we're born into it. The word translated "adoption" (*huiothesia*, literally "the placing of a son") is not referring to a child being placed (*thesia*) into a family but rather a child already in the family being placed into the authority of a fully matured son (*huios*).[2] It's about jurisdiction and rights, not entering the family.

The word *seed* in 1 Peter 1:23 is the same Greek term translated as "sperm" or "spore."[3] Any biologist knows that a discussion of genetics isn't complete without mentioning "seeds"—these are the means through which a species' nature is passed on. When we're born again, that is exactly what happens: God's life and nature are planted in us. In the same way we receive our DNA from our biological parents, we receive our spiritual DNA from our heavenly Father. It is planted in our spirit to grow and mature directly after His image.

Think about a plant's seed. Contained within it are the blueprints for what the baby plant is destined to be. The design is already there, as are all the essential schematics. Everything the plant-to-be needs to grow and be *just like* its parent plant is contained within the tiny seed.

EVERYTHING YOU NEED TO AGAIN BE IN THE IMAGE OF YOUR HEAVENLY FATHER IS GIVEN TO YOU THE MOMENT YOU ACCEPT CHRIST.

Likewise, everything you need to again be in the image of your heavenly Father is given to you the moment you accept Christ. Your spirit is loaded with God's DNA, His eternal life. Your destiny is secure. You are complete in Him (Colossians 2:10)—in your spirit. All you have to do from that point is *become outwardly who you already are inwardly!*

This is what the Bible is referring to when it talks about predestination, sometimes a touchy subject with Christians. Preconceived notions aside, the word—*proorizô*—simply means God has predetermined that you'd be like His Son, Jesus. *Pro* means "ahead of time"; *orizô* means "horizon or boundary."[4] God marks the boundaries of who we are ahead of time. He sets our horizons. He knows and plans our destiny. Doesn't that make you feel secure?

Paul uses another word for this in Ephesians, one I really love: *prothésis.*[5] "We have obtained an inheritance, having been predestined according to His *purpose* who works all things after the counsel of His will" (1:11). And, "This was in accordance with the eternal *purpose* which He carried out in Christ Jesus our Lord" (3:11). God has written the *thesis*—the purpose—for our lives before we ever come out of our mothers' womb. He has stamped us with His DNA by His Spirit. We are loved, accepted, whole, destined for great things in the kingdom ... the list is as long as His promises to us.

In the same way, "we are His workmanship, created in Christ Jesus for good works, which God *prepared beforehand* so that we would walk in them" (Ephesians 2:10). The emphasized term, in Greek, pictures a tailor measuring out dimensions to make a garment. If you've ever had a suit or dress made for you, what's the first thing your tailor or seamstress did? Measured you ... *precisely.* Arms, waist, shoulders, neck, legs ... every measurement carefully recorded to piece together a garment that fit you to a tee. Approximated measurements would produce a piece of clothing better suited for someone else. *Yours* is produced with you, and no one else, in mind.

That's what all these verses are describing. Your destiny is tailor-made by God. Fit exactly to His liking. He's marked your boundaries and horizons, written your thesis statement. He measured you fully, stamped His DNA all over your spirit, and then went to work forming what He's already designed you to be.

That's a Father who loves His child.

COMPLETELY, UTTERLY, ENTIRELY, 100 PERCENT NEW

As we've seen, Paul explains the result of having God's life within us: "Therefore if anyone is in Christ, he is a new creature; the old things passed away; behold, new things have come" (2 Corinthians 5:17). The term for "new," *kainos,* shows the extent to which God restores our fallen spirit. Sometimes, to get the full meaning of a word, it's just as important to know what it *isn't* as what it is. In this case, Paul could have used *neos,* which means *quantitatively* new, but instead used *kainos,* which denotes something *qualitatively* new. Let me illustrate the difference.

Not long ago our family needed a new computer. The old one was running slow, and the kids were getting frustrated with its overloaded memory and the modem's lagging connection. Ceci's first thought was to call up a techie buddy who helped us purchase the original one. He brought to our house a new motherboard that upgraded the memory, the modem, and a couple other things. But still, it was all housed within the same computer we had before. That's what would be described as *neos*. It was quantitatively new—not a different kind or a different quality, just new by means whereby it replaced the old one with the same basic computer.

Within two days, our buddy suggested another option. Though we were fine with the upgrade, he found a deal we couldn't pass up. For about the same price we were able to get a brand-new laptop with all the bells and whistles. It was faster, ran more smoothly, looked nicer . . . and we didn't even have to plug into a phone line anymore ("wi-fi," if you're a Neanderthal like me!). In Greek, we'd call this *kainos*. It wasn't the same computer, enhanced; it was of a completely new kind and quality.

> **YOU'RE BORN AGAIN EVERY DAY, IN A SENSE, AND THE ETERNAL LIFE IN YOUR SPIRIT IS ALWAYS NEW.**

When God declares us new creations, He's not saying we're refurbished sinners or reworked versions of what was already there. You're not just another person who's come down the assembly line of the remanufactured fallen. You're part of a new race (1 Peter 2:9) that takes directly after Jesus, the last Adam. And each of us in this new race is original. There's never before been anyone like you in the kingdom of God. You are a brand-spankin'-new creature.

In fact, 2 Corinthians 4:16 says we're "being renewed day by day." Once again, "renewed" is a *kainos* type of new, only this time Paul says our spirits are perpetually new—daily. It's a state of being, not a past tense. You're born again every day, in a sense, and the eternal life in your spirit is always new.

I'm being thorough and technical in pointing this out because I'm well aware of how many have a hard time accepting it. But it's true. *If you've been born again, you are a new creation.* No matter what you've done or where you've been, when you invite Christ into your heart, you are newer than new. Every day you're a clean, pure, holy image of His Son, Jesus—in your spirit.

You aren't just a "fixed" Christian. By God's Spirit in you, you're now a permanent Christ-ian, which means "little Christ." You're identical to the purest human being who ever walked the earth. On the inside, you're the twin of God's favorite person! Whereas before you had the nature of sin, darkness, rebellion, and, ultimately, death, now in your spirit you are essentially a walking Jesus. You're full of *zoé*. You are new.

That's grounds for celebration! Just don't jump the gun.

It Ain't Over Yet

Despite a stellar career, legendary jockey Willie Shoemaker will also be remembered for celebrating too soon at the 1957 Kentucky Derby. Ahead of the pack with mere yards to go, Shoemaker misjudged the finish line while riding Gallant Man and stood up in the stirrups, only to watch the Bill Hartack-run Iron Liege gallop past to claim first place.

No hard-core football fan can think of onetime Dallas Cowboy Leon Lett without remembering his boneheaded play on the game's most illustrious stage. During the fourth quarter of Super Bowl XXVII, Lett recovered a fumble and, on his way to a sure touchdown, extended his arms to celebrate before entering the end zone. Inches before he crossed the goal line, Buffalo receiver Don Beebe swooped in from behind and knocked the ball loose.[6]

Then there's what could be the most embarrassing hot-dogging incident in sports history. During the 2006 Winter Olympics, U.S. snowboarder Lindsey Jacobellis had made the finals of the snowboard-cross event. After surviving two crashes that had taken out two of her three competitors, she was far ahead and needed only to complete a few routine jumps before crossing the finish line. Collecting the gold was all but hers; the TV commentators were already remarking on what a perfect run she'd had.

But on her second-to-last jump, Jacobellis inexplicably attempted a backside-method grab in which she twisted in the air, grabbed her board, and was supposed to whirl back around for a smooth landing.

That didn't happen.

Instead, the Vermont native landed on the edge of her board and fell onto her back. Before she could recover, Swiss boarder Tanja Frieden flew past her and shockingly finished first. Though Jacobellis initially denied prematurely showboating—instead claiming she grabbed her board to maintain stability—she later admitted to getting caught up in the moment.[7]

HOME FREE? NOT QUITE

Similarly, it would be easy for us to jump the gun and indulge in a little hot-dogging at this point in our journey. After all, we've learned that not only has God made a way to restore us to our original state of perfection in Him, but as born-again Christians our spirits are already there. In God's eyes, we are completely accepted and perfect. No struggles. In fact, to Him we look just like His Son. Paul says that "in Him you have been made complete" (Colossians 2:10), while John adds that "of His fullness we have all received" (John 1:16). We've got Jesus' DNA, His *zoé*, His *Pneuma*. That at least deserves a little pre-end zone celebration, doesn't it?

Not so fast. Remember the "If I am, why don't I" question? We've only made it to the first half of it in our study—"If I am." As you consider the new you, let me remind you that all this wonderful news pertains to the spirit. Once again: When you're born again, your spirit is instantly renewed, but it's a different story with the soul. Your soul didn't get saved when your spirit did. And even though the state of your spirit mirrors Christ, *it is your soul that determines what you do and how you act.*

In other words, your unsaved soul is the deciding factor on whether or not that Christlikeness within you will be released out of your born-again spirit. (Your body will basically obey whatever your soul decides.) You're not yet a *pneumatikos* (spirit-controlled person); you're a *psuchikos* with *pneumatikos* potential. As one of the *Annie* orphans, Annie was prone to say, "Oh my goodness, oh my goodness!" Or perhaps Annie's favorite expression is in order: "Leapin' lizards!" The tattoos are still there!

> YOUR UNSAVED SOUL IS THE DECIDING FACTOR ON WHETHER OR NOT THAT CHRISTLIKENESS WITHIN YOU WILL BE RELEASED OUT OF YOUR BORN-AGAIN SPIRIT.

It's here that disillusionment sets in for so many—the "Why don't I?" part of the question. Often Christians have such high expectations of how things are supposed to be after conversion that when reality hits—the old thoughts return, former weaknesses continue to control, the patterns and strongholds of *psuché* still exist—faith begins to falter. Post-conversion reality, as we all know, doesn't always feel like a pillow-top mattress. (In my experience, it was more like head-on colliding with a Mack truck!)

James says we still must "receive the word implanted, which is able to save your souls" (1:21). Notice that he didn't say our soul was saved—it's now *able to be* saved. He makes the distinction of this being *a process.* Our spirit is saved; our soul has the *potential* of being saved. The same redeeming life of God that immediately transformed our spirit must now begin to transform our soul through the process of God's Word being grafted or implanted into it. I'll explain this process, but not yet. For now, we simply need to recognize its necessity.

YOUR SPIRIT IS NEW, YOUR SOUL IS BEING MADE NEW, AND YOUR BODY WILL BE MADE NEW WHEN YOU GET TO HEAVEN.

While you're already a new creation in your spirit, you're *becoming* a new creation in your soul. Big difference. Your spirit *is* new, your soul is *being made* new, and your body *will be made* new when you get to heaven. Take a look at the following chart, which recaps the state of each part of our being.

SPIRIT	SOUL	BODY
Reborn	Renewed	Regulated
Saved	Being saved	Will be saved
New	Being made new	Will be made new
What, who I am in Christ	Determines what I do and how I act	Will basically obey the soul
My standing legally	My state experientially	——
2 Corinthians 5:17	James 1:21	Romans 6–8
1 Peter 1:23	2 Corinthians 3:18	1 Corinthians 9:27

Both our *psuché* life, inherited from the fall, and our subconscious mind, with its strongholds and unwholesome memories, still exist.

These are the distinct soul elements that often refuse to acknowledge that God is in command and insist upon *psuché*'s continued enthronement and exaltation. This is why, even as "saved" Christians, we can still be struggling with our pride, wrestling with our quick temper, or grappling with our tendency to stretch the truth every now and then just to make us look good. We really are like a resurrected person still trapped in a tomb!

If our soul were already completely saved, then whatever God birthed in our spirit would come directly out through our soul. When the spirit (which doesn't struggle with faith) claims, "I believe!" our soul (which must see to believe) wouldn't instinctively say, "Prove it." When our spirit tries to emanate its Christlike self-control and self-discipline, the soul wouldn't sometimes react with a desire for more food, drugs, pornography ... whatever vice most compels us. And yet that's how it is. Our soul still carries our old nature, while the spirit has already received the new. We're still a mess between the ears.

If you had a stronghold in your soul before conversion, it can absolutely still exist after conversion.✝ If you struggled with pornography or drugs or anger in your BC (Before Christ) days, even though the presence of the life and Spirit of God within you has now cleansed and freed your spirit, your soul can still struggle with these appetites and is still infected by its exalted and sinful nature.

None of this means we should question the reality of our salvation—that isn't in doubt. It simply explains the two-way traffic that seems to be going on inside us. We're saved *and* being saved.

✝Obviously, there are plenty of exceptions, which is why we hear wonderful "God instantly delivered me from my addiction" stories. Praise God for His miraculous saving power! My personal belief is that, more often than not, these radical deliverances are connected to how fully a person received *and understood* the message of the cross, repentance, forgiveness, cleansing, etc., which we'll touch on later.

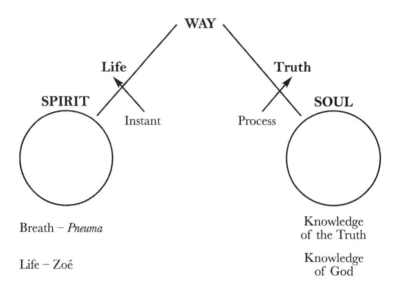

Breath – *Pneuma*

Life – Zoé

Knowledge
of the Truth

Knowledge
of God

STEP BY STEP . . . AND HERE ARE THE FIRST ONES

Since our spirit's rebirth is instant and complete, while our soul's is not, we must be committed to the *process* of transforming our soul. Second Corinthians 3:18, which we've read before, describes this as a

> **WE MUST BE COMMITTED TO THE PROCESS OF TRANSFORMING OUR SOUL.**

process of "being *transformed* into the same image from glory to glory, just as from the Lord, the Spirit."

This word *transformed* is from *metamorphoô*, which (as I'm sure you've already guessed) is where we get *metamorphosis*. A good definition is "the process of change from one form or state to another *from the inside out*"—like the butterfly.[8] Her DNA didn't change; she just had to become what she already was. In the same manner, we aren't changed into Christ's likeness from the soul inward but from our spirit outward. *We must become who we are.*

Ephesians confirms this and outlines the process:

> In reference to your former manner of life, you lay aside the old self, which is being corrupted in accordance with the lusts of deceit, and that you be renewed in the spirit of your mind, and put on the new self, which in the likeness of God has been created in righteousness and holiness of the truth. (4:22–24)

Paul speaks again of this transformation process from the inside out (this metamorphosis):

> Therefore I urge you, brethren, by the mercies of God, to present your bodies a living and holy sacrifice, acceptable to God, which is your spiritual service of worship. And do not be conformed to this world, but be transformed [*metamorphoō*] by the renewing of your mind, so that you may prove what the will of God is, that which is good and acceptable and perfect. (Romans 12:1–2)

A caterpillar doesn't strive to become a butterfly. She doesn't stress or fret over the matter. She simply begins the process of chrysalis, waits inside her hardened, cocoon-like outer layer, and rests. And the natural progression, the logical outcome, is that she becomes what the blueprints inside her already declared she would be. And so it is with us. We already are—on the inside! Now we must become . . . who we are.

If You're a King, Then Be a King

I can't imagine a better example of someone becoming who he already was than Aragorn in Tolkien's *Lord of the Rings*. In case you're one of the few who haven't read the books, seen the movies, or caught wind of the story through the cultural hype, I'll give you the Cliffs-Notes version.

In the fantasy world of Middle Earth, Aragorn is the last remaining descendent of a former king who ruled the kingdom of Gondor. In other words, he's the only rightful heir left to a now-empty throne. Following the death of his father when he was two, Aragorn's mother placed him in hiding for fear he'd be killed by those who knew his identity—just like his father and grandfather. Yet even when he became an adult, and this identity was revealed to him by his guardians, Aragorn remained too fearful to assume a king's responsibilities. Instead, he opted to live in the shadows as a ranger who roamed the lands.

It's at this point that the trilogy picks up Aragorn's story. And while the adventures of four hobbits, a dwarf, an elf, a wizard, and a couple of humans fill the pages, this kingly subplot becomes key to the survival (and longevity) of the entire world. After years of running and hiding, Aragorn finally gains the courage to face his fears, declares himself the rightful heir of Isildur, and, after confronting Middle Earth's wicked dark lord, ascends the throne. He even takes on his rightfully given name, Elessar, and reigns as ruler of a united kingdom.

We don't have to wait generations to assume the identity of who God says we already are. Just as Aragorn finally accepted his true calling, we can as well. Our *psuché* will constantly seek to haunt us with reminders of a sinful nature. It will try to render us ineffective by creating fear over all the "what ifs." Yet Paul reminds us that we can resist the fallen world's allure—which preys on our unsaved soul—and be transformed from the inside out.

"Do not be conformed to this world," he says. The word *conformed* is from *suschematizô* (this is where we get *schematic*), which literally means "to be fashioned together with."[9] Don't let the world tell you what your schematic is or what you're supposed to be. Refuse to be fashioned from the outside in. Do not be shaped by what happened to you in a bad relationship or by how you gave yourself to a sinful habit. Don't take on the blueprints that the world around you and your past experiences have drawn, but instead be transformed from within—*metamorphoô*—like the caterpillar into a butterfly.

As if he were putting a cherry on top, Paul continues by saying that once we've done all this—offered our beings as living sacrifices, rejected the world's blueprints, and transformed our minds—then we'll prove God's will. What does this mean? The word translated *prove* actually means "to demonstrate" something.[10] God is encouraging us that as this process occurs, we will bring forth a demonstration of what His will for us really is. He knows what is inside of us; He put it there. Now He wants to draw it out from our *pneuma* into our *psuché*.

COUNTING THE COST

Allow me to pause and speak directly to your heart, if you will. At this point we're facing a crossroad, and anytime you approach a crossroad, it's good to have a word of encouragement.

> When Andy Griffith, star of the classic television program that bore his name, entered his fifties, he found it increasingly difficult to find work in Hollywood, and his personal finances became tighter and tighter. He wrote in *Guideposts* that finally he and his wife, Cindi, decided things would be easier if they moved from Los Angeles back to Andy's home state of North Carolina; so they put their home up for sale and waited for a buyer. Unfortunately, the real estate market was down, and no one gave them a decent offer. Months passed, and Andy grew depressed.

Then one day the Lord gave Cindi an insight. "Maybe it's a good thing we couldn't sell the house," she said. "Maybe it was God showing us grace. If we moved to North Carolina now, you might indeed never work again. What we need to do is stay here and stoke the fire."

And stoke the fire they did. Day after day they went together to the office of the talent agency that represented Andy. They sat in the lobby, chatted with agents, and went with them to lunch. Eventually the work started to come in: four TV movies that year, including the pilot for *Matlock*, a show that ended up running for nine years.[11]

Griffith stuck with it, thanks to his wife's perceptiveness. And the results speak for themselves, as he went on to further cement his status as a legendary actor and all-round good guy. It took commitment to perseverance, however, before he reached the other side.

Is it any different when dealing with our efforts to overcome the soulish nature? Getting to the point where our entire being is completely spirit-dominated—going from being a *psuchikos* to a *pneumatikos*—takes commitment. It takes perseverance. And it certainly takes the patience and grace to continue through the times when we fall back to our soul's tendencies. But God is determined to see you completely controlled by Him—with your spirit guiding and your soul serving.

He will not fail in His mission. He will see you through to completion. Do you have a part in it? You bet. Can you sabotage the job? Unfortunately, yes, since God will not force His transformation on you. But as long as you purpose in your heart that your Maker will have His way, you are in the cocoon. As long as you allow His Spirit to have its way and grow in influence through your life, you will fly. It's time to become a butterfly.

It's time to see the blueprints become reality.

It's time to become you!

CHAPTER 8

YOU'VE GOT TO BE KIDDING ME

Isn't there another way?

I'm convinced that has to be one of the most frequently asked questions during times that have made a permanent mark on human history.

When an aging Abraham was instructed by God to offer his long-awaited son, Isaac, as a sacrifice on the altar (the same boy who was the apparent fulfillment of God's promise to make Abraham a father of many nations), it's likely the thought crossed his mind more than once as he journeyed up that mountain: "Lord, isn't there another way?"

When God instructed Gideon to take only three hundred men (out of 32,000) into battle against a 135,000-strong Midianite army, I wouldn't doubt the leader considered the odds (Israel was outnumbered 450 to one), choked backed disbelief, and tempered his "Are you crazy?!" reaction with a sincere "Isn't there another way?"

When Mohandas Gandhi led thousands of oppressed citizens against the ruling British empire in both South Africa and India through nonviolent civil disobedience, the threats of beatings, arrests, and general hardship likely had more than a few of his countrymen asking, "Isn't there another way?"

Likewise, when Martin Luther King Jr. was thrown into prison for defying yet another unjust Jim Crow law, the thought probably crossed the minds of those closest to him: "Isn't there another way?"

History books are filled with examples of those who have stood up against a foe—in whatever form—knowing full well they would be maligned, persecuted, even killed. It's a tremendous task to fight for something bigger than yourself. And yet no one faced a more unavoidable, hideous enemy than did Jesus Christ. His entire life purpose was to give this enemy a fatal blow. He left the indescribable glory of His heavenly throne just to put this adversary down for the count.

Still, when Jesus faced the daunting mission of going to the cross, He too wondered aloud, "Isn't there another way?" (see Matthew 26:39). Here was the Son of God, who'd done nothing but follow His Father's plans to absolute perfection, who'd lived every single moment in denial of His own will . . . here Jesus was pleading to His Father for a way out.

But there was no other way. And as we'll see, the cross was all about the exalted *psuché*. Here we start to learn how the process of transforming the soul begins. It should actually start in each of us the moment we accept Christ as Savior, but it doesn't always, partly because of a deficient gospel message. If this has been your experience, if the transforming of your soul hasn't taken place as it should have, know that this is about to change.

My words in this chapter are not easy to put forward, and they're going to offend exalted *psuché*. If at any point I sound as if I don't want your soul to be healed but rather made to feel worse, be assured that isn't the case. They simply must be stated. The fact that they so often go unsaid is the reason many of us are still *psuchikoses* (soul-ruled) rather than *pneumatikoses* (spirit-ruled). The truth is, the way to live is to die, and before we're finished you'll understand what God meant by this. Fasten your seat belt, this could be a bumpy ride.

This Is Our Guy?!

Only our Maker could provide the solution for our problem—we can't save or heal ourselves—so Jesus came to reverse the curse brought on by man's fall. Obviously, this was no insignificant curse but one brought on by the greatest enemy to God's intended path for man: spiritual death and an exalted soul. It was what caused the first human to lose communion with his Maker, and it would be humanity's eternal death knell without someone stepping in to save the day.

Enter our Savior . . . in disguise.

Jesus didn't come exactly as man expected or wanted. There was no national holiday to celebrate His arrival. He didn't come floating down from heaven with fanfare and fireworks or laser lights and pyrotechnics (though the shepherds who saw and heard the angels announce His birth may beg to differ).

Instead, Jesus began His life on earth exactly the way He ended it: in complete humility. Humanity wanted a king; He came as a servant. We wanted a general in the army; He came as a foot soldier. Everything—can I emphasize this enough?—*everything* Jesus did grated against our proud, exalted *psuché*. He was born in a manger—an animal trough, for goodness' sake! He didn't own a house; in fact, from every biblical indication, it's doubtful Jesus owned anything but the clothes on His back. And instead of proving all His enemies wrong with one vengeful "I'll show you" action, He accepted being mocked, spit upon, ridiculed, and scorned.

Why would Jesus do it this way? Because every facet of His life—from birth to death and everything in between—was designed to reverse the fall, where pride entered and *psuché* was exalted. *Psuché* would have wanted—no, our *psuché*-nature expected—opulence and charisma. A poster-boy Savior.

But we got a Redeemer whom the Bible describes as having "no beauty or majesty to attract us to him, nothing in his appearance that we should desire him" (Isaiah 53:2 NIV). No glitz. No glamour. Even His hometown was suspect (Mark 6:1–6). The guy whom *psuché* expected never showed up.

Great plan, huh?

Under a Higher Order

Instead of irresistible features, a head-turning stature, or a cosmic ego, Jesus had what counted most: obedience. In fact, He never did a single thing without first receiving word from His Father.

> The Son can do nothing of Himself, unless it is something He sees the Father doing; for whatever the Father does, these things the Son also does in like manner. (John 5:19)

Think maybe Jesus was exaggerating just a bit when He said this? Think again. When soul-dominated doubters came and asked Christ for signs and wonders, He wouldn't lift a finger unless His Father instructed Him to do so. Not a single miracle was performed in His ministry that wasn't ordained by the Father, because He was reversing Adam's decision to exalt man's own will and knowledge. When Satan tempted Jesus in the wilderness, the enemy's primary goal wasn't to get God's Son to show him nifty miracles he'd never seen. He wanted Christ to exalt His *psuché*—to fall into the same trap that snared the first Adam—and be disqualified as our Redeemer.

The devil wanted Him to defy His Father, to do something on His own initiative, just once: *Work a miracle on your own volition. Exalt your will. Make some decisions with your personal, human wisdom. Just do something to exalt self—psuché—above your spirit.*

Not on His life. Literally . . . that would not happen once. He came to do God's will, and God's will alone (Hebrews 10:5–7). Again, He was reversing the actions of Adam, whose soul came out of submission to His Maker and declared he would do things his own way. Christ was on an uncompromising mission, and no one would stop Him. Not Satan, not those wanting proof He was Messiah, not His own mother, not His beloved disciples. Someone had to bring *psuché*—self-will—off the throne, and there was only one human who could possibly do it.

> **SOMEONE HAD TO BRING PSUCHÉ—SELF-WILL—OFF THE THRONE, AND THERE WAS ONLY ONE HUMAN WHO COULD POSSIBLY DO IT.**

When Jesus had been laying out His plans on deaf ears, Peter felt the force of His determination by unwittingly trying to get Him to honor *psuché* over *pneuma.*

> From that time Jesus began to show His disciples that He must go to Jerusalem, and suffer many things from the elders and chief priests and scribes, and be killed, and be raised up on the third day.
>
> Peter took Him aside and began to rebuke Him [a very harsh Greek word, used primarily for rebuking demons], saying, "God forbid it, Lord! This shall never happen to You" (Matthew 16:21–22).

Notice that Peter "took Him aside." Wasn't it nice of Peter not to rebuke Jesus in front of the others? After all, everyone knows that if you're ever going to reprimand God's Son, you should do it in private.

Take Him aside like talk-first, think-later Peter and bring the correction: "Now, listen, Lord. You're deceived. Let me straighten You out on this."

Man, did Peter get an earful. And not necessarily because he was reprimanding God Almighty. What angered Jesus was the satanically inspired *psuché* within Peter trying to sidetrack Him into softening up His soul-killing plan. You see—and you must!—when Jesus spoke of going to the cross, He was always referring to taking *psuché* there. Not once did He use the word for physical life (*bios*) when speaking of laying down His "life," although that was necessary and would happen. Nor did He use *zoé*—He wasn't laying that down. "Life" was always the word *psuché*—the soul. Jesus always, without exception, spoke of laying down *psuché*.

Translated literally, Peter's statement reads, "Have mercy on Your*self*, Jesus." Jesus knew what this would mean: mercy on *psuché*.

His immediate response? None! No mercy for *psuché*—it's destined for the cross!

> He turned and said to Peter, "Get behind Me, Satan! You
> are a stumbling block to Me; for you are not setting your
> mind on God's interests, but man's" (Matthew 16:23).

Ouch. Not only did Jesus call out Peter's devil-birthed suggestion, He explained why it was in direct opposition to God. Peter's vision was pleasing the soul, doing what felt and seemed right. In his eyes, Jesus needed to overthrow the Romans, set up His earthly throne, and prove He was the long-awaited Ruler. The protocol for a *psuché* plan: satisfy exalted *psuché*. Exalt it some more—don't kill it.

Jesus would have none of it. He knew that the only way He could roll away the weight of death and the stone guarding the grave was to crucify *psuché*.

Again, even at the most opportune time for Jesus to give in—when He was praying in Gethsemane—He stayed strong. While He was in unimaginable anguish over His looming task of suffering for our sins, we can see in every gospel account how the battle was also over laying down versus saving His soul—His own will.

"My soul is deeply grieved to the point of death," He told the disciples (Mark 14:34). His soul—yes, His *psuché*—was clamoring to be heard over His spirit. He even pleaded, "My Father, if it is possible, let this cup pass from Me" (Matthew 26:39). You can hear His soul wrestling, coming up with any sort of alternative, fighting for its life. Finally, His spirit won: "Yet not as I will, but as You will."

That is fall-reversal talk! With it, our *psuché* took a knife to the heart.

Whereas the first Adam chose to disobey God and seek His own knowledge of good and evil, Christ came to obey and follow God's *logos*—His word, will, and ways—to the letter. He laid down what Adam took up. Jesus would not cater to *psuché* or satisfy its desires, even at the cost of death. Why did He unfailingly refuse to do anything of His own volition? Because He was laying down *psuché*—reversing our original sin and bringing the soul back under the control of the Spirit and the Father.

That was the plan. The good news. Jesus took *psuché* to the cross and conquered it once and for all.

A JOINT VENTURE

Now for the not-so-great news: If we want to participate in that victory, Jesus says we must go there too. Our *psuché* must die. Not literally, but self-will, born at the fall, must be put to death. In John 12:24–25, He stated it this way:

Truly, truly, I say to you, unless a grain of wheat falls into the earth and dies, it remains alone; but if it dies, it bears much fruit.

He who loves his *life* loses it, and he who hates his *life* in this world will keep it to *life* eternal.

There are three mentions of "life" in this one verse. Without knowing the Greek words used, you could not possibly grasp Christ's meaning. The first two, as you might guess, are *psuché:* "He who loves his *psuché* loses it, and he who hates his *psuché* in this world will keep it. . . ." The last one, however, is *zoé*—eternal life. In other words, if you're going to live for your soul, you're going to lose it. You must hate the life of the soul to receive the life of the spirit, the eternal life that represents God's fullness.

> **YOU MUST HATE THE LIFE OF THE SOUL TO RECEIVE THE LIFE OF THE SPIRIT, THE ETERNAL LIFE THAT REPRESENTS GOD'S FULLNESS.**

At this point, let me say a word about strongholds. While this chapter and the next deal primarily with God's plan for *psuché*, much of the latter part of this book deals specifically with how to overcome strongholds. For now, it's important that we first see how Christ's provision dealt with the exalting of *psuché*, which is what created the potential for strongholds. It's after we've comprehended how God's life begins its saving work on the soul that we can deal with our strongholds.

Remember the harsh words Jesus said when Peter suggested He have mercy on Himself? The Lord immediately followed it by telling all the disciples,

> If anyone wishes to come after Me, he must deny himself, and take up his cross and follow Me. For whoever wishes to save his life [*psuché*] will lose it; but whoever loses his life [*psuché*] for My sake will find it. For what will it profit a man if he gains the whole world and forfeits his soul [*psuché*]? Or what will a man give in exchange for his soul [*psuché*]? (Matthew 16:24–26)

To go after Jesus, we must deny our *psuché*, take up our cross, and follow Him. Where? To the cross. It's only there that we find *zoé*. Christ's sacrificial work was in one sense substitutionary, but in another sense He insists we go there too. Only by doing so can we begin to experience the fruit of our born-again spirit into our soul.

We Christians have missed this so pathetically it is heretical. For most of us, if we entertain the concept at all, taking up our cross means either suffering for Christ or allowing Him to be in charge of our life. These are *results*, and results that few ever really attain, because we miss His point. Jesus was saying, "If you really want *zoé* life to be operational again, *psuché* must die! It must come down from its exalted place, and the life-force that entered into it at the fall must go to the cross." This is what making Jesus our Lord—giving Him charge of our life—is all about. But most believers never experience it. They won't even tithe (give to God the first tenth of their income), much less put *everything* under His control. Why? Because exaltation of self is still alive and well.

Interestingly, the Greek word translated "take up" (our cross) is *airô*, the one used in 2 Corinthians 10:5 when Paul says we should cast down every "lofty thing *raised up* against the knowledge of God." We're either going to exalt the cross of Christ or exalt our knowledge, the *psuché*, above God's. One leads to living life primarily from the soul, the other to doing so from the spirit.

A Fool's Cross

To unbelievers, exalting our Savior's merciless humiliation and vicious slaughter seems anything but smart. It offends intellectual *psuché*. Often, the more intellectual a person is the more ridiculous the message of the cross appears to be.

Paul writes explicitly about this in 1 Corinthians 1:18–25:

> The word [*logos*] of the cross is foolishness [literally, "moronic"] to those who are perishing, but to us who are being saved [there's that process!] it is the power of God. For it is written, "I will destroy the wisdom of the wise, and the cleverness of the clever I will set aside."
>
> Where is the wise man? Where is the scribe? Where is the debater of this age? Has not God made foolish the wisdom of the world?
>
> For since *in the wisdom of God the world through its wisdom did not come to know God*, God was well-pleased through the foolishness of the message preached [a savior on a cross] to save those who believe. For indeed Jews ask for signs and Greeks search for wisdom [*psuché!*]; but we preach Christ crucified, to Jews a stumbling block [literally "scandalous"] and to Gentiles foolishness ["moronic"], but to those who are the called, both Jews and Greeks, Christ the power of God and the wisdom of God. Because the foolishness of God is wiser than men, and the weakness of God is stronger than men.

What amazing revelation of God's glorious plan! Foolish? Only to our foolish minds. Paul speaks of the message (*logos*) of the cross being the power of God to those who are being saved. Though utterly ridiculous to those who are lost, it contains God's power to save for those who hear and believe.

In His wisdom, God knew He couldn't let the world come to know

Him through its own wisdom. That would simply further exalt *psuché*—the "wisdom" originating in *psuché* only feeds its pride.

No, *psuché* can't save *psuché*. *Psuché* has to die! We "wise" humans think we can save ourselves, preaching a gospel of works, seeking to earn our way to divine favor and redemption. Or we invent some other religion with a man-made method of salvation. Essentially, it's all about what *we* can do, rather than what *God* has done. The results, however, do nothing but reinforce the problem: an exalted soul that becomes even more elevated.

So God worked humility into the process—nonnegotiable humilty. When we humble ourselves, we receive grace. When we exalt ourselves, God resists us (James 4:6).

God's way compels the soul to humble itself and relinquish its power at the cross. And the cross, again, is "moronic" to humanity. Who would

> **GOD'S WAY COMPELS THE SOUL TO HUMBLE ITSELF AND RELINQUISH ITS POWER AT THE CROSS.**

claim a crucified man to be a hero, much less a savior? What kind of power lets itself be tortured and murdered? As Paul says, it's an offense, a "stumbling block." The original word is *skandalon*, from which comes *scandal*.

A *skandalon* was the trigger on a trap set for animals; in fact, some translators define the word as a "trap stick."[1] It was the stick to which bait was attached—raw meat hung on a stick or tied to a string. When an animal came along and took the bait, the trap would be triggered and the animal would be captured.

In a scandal, someone takes the bait—does something he shouldn't and ends up trapped. Paul's use of this term is an ingenious play on words. Think about it: What's the bait on a stick? Jesus on the cross. Literally a piece of raw, bloody meat dangling before ravenous, bloodthirsty hunters. That this could be the way to salvation is scandalous, an incomprehensible stumbling block to arrogant, high and mighty *psuché*.

That's exactly why God chose to do it this way. He wants to humble *psuché*, not appeal to it, and no part of the true cross message does appeal to it. Apart from having the Spirit's revelation, the message of the cross is idiotic—especially the part about our identification with it. To the Greeks who valued wisdom, it was senseless and foolish. To the Jews, who held that anyone who was hung on a tree was cursed and defiled (Deuteronomy 21:22–23), it was humiliating and offensive. Yet that's exactly what God wanted it to be, to the soul: a stench that would offend and humble *psuché*, constraining man to come to God only on His terms. Everything about the cross was designed to bring the soul off its lofty throne. *Psuché* didn't like it and still doesn't.

> **EVERYTHING ABOUT THE CROSS WAS DESIGNED TO BRING THE SOUL OFF ITS LOFTY THRONE.**

GOSPEL LITE

When's the last time a preacher's sermon offended you to the point of disgust? Can you remember your soul ever feeling humiliated and ashamed during a service? Probably not. If you've lived long in the U.S., you've been exposed to the evolution of a salvation message far removed from the vile cross. We do not preach a message that allows God to break or kill *psuché*. Instead, we try to be appealing to it. We prefer a gospel couched in plush surroundings with a feel-good ending that gives us the tinglies. Hey, why don't we make church just like a formula film? Let's have an entertainment break from life and sit in stadium seats while a slick preacher tells us all is right with the universe and God exists only to bless us on request.

I'm only being facetious to a degree. I see no problem with appealing to a postmodern generation high on stimulation. But unfortunately, to compete with the onslaught of entertainment doused out by the world, the church has tinkered with the gospel. Updated, modulated, refined, pleasant, relevant . . . call it what you will, *we've removed the offense of the cross* and in so doing have removed its power. No wonder there's such little transformation at most conversions. We're so desperate to see results that we've diluted the message. We preach to *psuché*, through *psuché*, and wonder why we don't change *psuché*. We try to be appealing to *psuché* and wonder why he doesn't die. It's because we offer him the wrong bait!

God help us all. Through watering it down, the gospel has become virtually unrecognizable within a generation's time. We've refused to tell the truth, the whole truth, and nothing but the truth: that the message of the cross is not only Christ dying there, it's also our placing our *psuché* there, laying our lives down. Otherwise, *psuché* remains enthroned in place of Jesus.

Unfortunately, because we function so much from *psuché* and package our message to be attractive to *psuché*, what we really preach is a humanistic what's-in-it-for-me gospel. *You want abundant life? You want to go to heaven when you die? You want God to become your partner and do wonderful things for you?* Those are appeals to pacify and satisfy self! We "bait" unbelievers not with the offense of the cross but with what they can gain from the deal. We remove the affront because we don't want to offend *psuché*—the very thing the cross was designed to do.

Pastors, I don't care if you have *seeker-sensitive* services as long as you have *psuché-sanitizing* messages. (I have yet to see the two combined.) Most of the time, however, we do seeker-sensitive meetings (which, basically, is designing a meeting for sinners) and water down the message because we want to see numbers and results. I contend, however, that if we preached the true message of the cross, God's power would be released in such a way that we would soon see the numbers of converts we desire.

The recent Brownsville Revival in Pensacola, Florida, didn't dilute the message in an attempt to be attractive to fallen *psuché*. They preached the straightforward, uncompromising gospel, and God's power showed up in extraordinary ways. They probably had more people saved in five years than all America's seeker-sensitive churches put together.

You won't find the what's-in-it-for-me gospel message in the New Testament. Jesus didn't preach it, Paul didn't preach it, the early church didn't preach it. The Lord never once tried to be appealing to *psuché*. Remember the rich young ruler who asked what he could do to receive eternal life (Luke 18:18–25)? Jesus mentioned a few command-ments—not His final answer, by the way—and the man perked up: "You'll be glad to know I've done everything you said ever since I was a kid," his *psuché* said, with its chest puffed out. Then Jesus dropped the bomb: "Oh, and one more thing . . . go sell everything you have and give the money to the poor, then come follow Me."

The ruler's *psuché* probably had a conniption, as my mom would say. "When he had heard these things, he became very sad [that would be *psuché*!], for he was extremely rich" (v. 23). Most of us today would have tapped the guy's shoulder as he was walking away and given him our best sales pitch. Appeal to *psuché*—quickly! "Um, excuse me, sir . . . you *do* know that if you give it all away for Jesus, He'll give you a hundred times as much in return?!?" We'd do all we could to make sure *psuché* stays comfortable and number one.

The problem is, a humanistic gospel produces humanistic con-verts; a diluted message produces diluted believers. It's all about *me*! America is full of them. *Psuchikos* Christians. Entertain them and they're happy. Talk about laying down their lives for Jesus, about sac-rifice, about denying the flesh, about obedience, about working to help fulfill the Great Commission ... and they're gone. Why should we be surprised? We didn't preach death to self-will; we baited them with heaven, forgiveness, and blessings. Certainly these are benefits of salvation, but we tried to bypass the cause in our rush to the effect. And now—God, help us!—we have a generation of humanistic, self-serving Christians.

Jesus isn't interested in our coming to Him on our own terms, with our soul still on its throne. His message is always the same: Lay it all down, come, and follow Me.

Take Your Time to Grieve

To do this, to become a true disciple of Christ, requires repentance. This, tragically, is yet another area of the gospel we're guilty of distorting. Part of the reason is our misunderstanding of true repentance.

If I asked a roomful of churchgoers to define repentance, it's likely at least 90 percent would tell me it means to turn and go the opposite way.

Wrong. Incomplete, at the very least.

At this point there are two related words we must grasp, both of which we must consider in light of what happened to our soul at the fall. One is *repentance*, the other is *revelation*.

Revelation is *apokalupsis* (you can hear *apocalypse* in it), which literally means "to remove [*apo*] a veil or covering [*kalupsis*], exposing to open view what was before hidden."[2] Why do we need this? Because something happened to our mind at the fall, shutting it off from being able to see knowledge or truth from God's perspective. When we chose our own, it blinded us to His. When the Holy Spirit "lifts the veil"—revelation—we see things once again from God's point of view.

When this process occurs, we now have repentance, *metanoia*, which literally means "new [*meta*] knowledge [*noia*]."[3] Again, see the connection to the fall: there we began walking according to our own knowledge; now, through revelation, we have a new knowledge (repentance). Does this involve turning and going the opposite way? Yes—but without a download of revelation and repentance from the Lord, our turning is simply a mental process still rooted in *psuché* and doesn't result in God's power being released to us. This is why our fruit is often temporary. We end up telling God we're sorry . . . again and again and again and again.

We often equate repentance with sorrow (or remorse), but they're not the same. The latter is the word *metamellomai*, which isn't biblical repentance and doesn't usually produce lasting change. Judas had *metamellomai* (Matthew 27:3); he was sorry for what he'd done but didn't experience true repentance.

There is a sorrow that can *lead to* repentance. Paul said,

> The sorrow that is according to the will of God produces
> a repentance without regret, leading to salvation, but the
> sorrow of the world produces death. (2 Corinthians 7:10)

Again, sorrow alone is not repentance, but it can be a part of the process.

As a pastor, I'm afraid I'm as guilty as anyone in allowing this to become an accepted misunderstanding. It's symptomatic of our times that leaders watch multitudes come to salvation only to walk away with their *psuché* barely touched, or, worse, still intact. Thinking that repentance is merely to turn and go the other way, people make a mental decision to do so and miss a crucial part of the process, which is the Spirit bringing revelation about their fallen condition. It's like a child apologizing to his parent without ever realizing what he actually did. The power of repentance lies in our seeing the true nature of our *psuché*, then receiving the Spirit's understanding and empowerment to take *psuché* to the cross, where it's put to death. If the unveiling and new knowledge—revelation and repentance—doesn't include the cross, where *psuché* dies and loses control, it is incomplete.

Evangelist Charles Finney understood this. He would often take time—four, five, six nights—during a revival before he ever gave an altar call. He was known to have grown men leap up and run to the altar during his sermons, weeping and crying for mercy, at which time he did the unthinkable: he politely sent them back to their seats. He knew they hadn't experienced true repentance yet.

Yes, they were sorry. Yes, to a degree they recognized their need for salvation. But until the Holy Spirit revealed to them the fullness of their condition, giving them a completely new understanding from God's perspective, their commitment to turning away would have been soul-powered and therefore temporary. At the very least, their transformation would have been minimal.

So Finney waited before he invited people to receive Christ. He would often purposely situate the room where prayer for salvation took place two or three blocks away from where he preached, just to compel new believers to be that much surer of the decision they were making. The results speak for themselves: 97 percent of Finney's converts became true disciples. (To put this in perspective, in our day I've heard estimates as low as 5 percent, regarding the number of our so-called converts that truly become Jesus-followers.)

When I was studying at Christ for the Nations, one elderly speaker, Charles Duncombe, would come and teach every year for a week. During one session he told us of an incident at his church in England. A man had come to the altar completely distraught, weeping and crying out what a terrible person he'd been, begging God for mercy. Within minutes, several members began huddling around him and saying things such as, "It's okay, it's okay. Jesus loves you and He forgives you. It's okay. . . ."

Seeing the scenario unfold, Duncombe sprinted over and quickly told them to stop. "Leave him alone," he instructed. Then he turned to the grieving man and said, "That's right, mourn over your condition. Grieve." And he left him in that state for almost three hours. (Maybe that's why generations ago they called the altar the "mourner's bench.") Then he began to comfort the man.

To our seeker-sensitive, soul-pleasing mindset, this seems rather harsh, especially given that the man was obviously sorry for the sins of his past. Yet this wise leader was sensitive enough to know that the Spirit was not finished with the work of revelation and repentance.

The Obvious Solution

Our *psuché* is no fan of true repentance. When we give the Spirit freedom to push aside old beliefs with new revelation, we're cleansing out the old soulish nature, essentially placing it on the cross to be crucified. If you haven't already gathered, it's *not* a fun process. Our soul doesn't enjoy taking a backseat after being at the wheel for so long. More often than not, our mind quickly begins to wonder if there's an alternative.

In *The Essential Calvin and Hobbes* by Bill Watterson, young Calvin says to his tiger friend, Hobbes, "I feel bad that I called Susie names and hurt her feelings. I'm sorry I did it."

"Maybe you should apologize to her," Hobbes suggests.

Calvin ponders this for a moment and replies, "I keep hoping there's a less obvious solution."[4]

Undoubtedly, our *psuché* wishes there were a less obvious solution than repentance and the cross. Maybe there's a way in which just *part* of the soul could remain in charge? We want the spirit-led life, but how about just a little soul left behind for good measure?

Read any portion of the Gospels and you'll see Jesus responding to that with a resounding "No!" There is no other way. No mercy for *psuché*! We must be willing to go to the cross, to lay down our *psuché*—our life—so that we may gain God's eternal *zoé*.

Stephen, Joan of Arc, William Wallace, John Brown, Gandhi, Martin Luther King ... all left a mark on the world by forfeiting their physical lives for their convictions. Each faced the same question: *Isn't there another way?* Jesus faced it too. Once more, for Him, the answer was "No!"

So it is for us. *Psuché* must go to the cross.

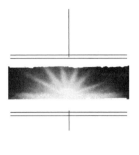

CHAPTER 9

EVERY DAY, IT'S A-GETTIN' CLOSER

In May 2005, a London motorist became the first man on earth to physically be in two different places at the same time.

At least that's what his city council claimed.

Colin Southwell first discovered his amazing feat when he received in the mail a ticket fining him £100. Along with the usual paper work was a freeze-frame photograph proving that at 9:47 A.M. on a certain weekday, he had driven his van in a buses-only lane. Busted. Verdict rendered.

That is, until he received a second ticket days later. This time, he was being charged with letting the meter expire on his parking spot. According to the ticket—another £100 fine—his offense had taken place at 9:48 A.M. on the exact same day as his previous misdeed. At a location several miles away.

How's that for driving fast?

Turns out, Southwell wasn't the amazingly speedy commuter people thought. No time travel here. A parking attendant wrongfully wrote a ticket before the Londoner's meter had actually run out and hoped he'd forget about the details by the time his ticket arrived via post. The city council admitted the obvious error and canceled his second ticket, promising to investigate and possibly penalize the parking contractor.[1]

Being in two places at the same time may seem impossible for the average Joe, but in a sense that's what Jesus calls believers to do in the battle between the spirit and the soul. Didn't you know? A little-known gift of the Spirit is teleportation.

Of course I'm joking. But when Christ instructed us to follow Him to the cross with *psuché* in tow, He was not joking. And it gets worse. He said we would have to go there every day: "If anyone wishes to come after Me, he must deny himself, and take up his cross *daily* and follow Me" (Luke 9:23). *Psuché* must remain at the cross!

God had four thousand years to plan the soul's new home. And did He ever plan well. He painted pictures of it through Old Testament types and shadows, spoke of it through veiled prophecies—which no one really figured out until after the fact—and even implemented a religious system that would symbolically depict it through myriad blood sacrifices. But even as the sacrificial Lamb showed up, no one expected Him to pass such a cruel sentence on the instigator of humanity's fall, the soul.

But what seemed like such an act of cruelty was at the same time an act of mercy. As we'll see in this and the next chapter, God is actually trying to return the soul to the restful condition it enjoyed before the rebellion. Basically, we must pitch our tent at the cross so our soul can RIP—rest in peace.

If we make the cross our soul's home, our spirit can live at the empty tomb! This is figurative, but the ensuing fruit is not.

It's Camping Time!

We've learned that triumphing over our fallen *psuché* was not a onetime deal. Yes, Jesus accomplished absolute and permanent victory for us over our exalted soul, but our experiencing of this will be a progressive journey. The adventure (of victory over our exalted soul) involves following Christ to the cross every single day. It's there that the peace, joy, and all the benefits of our salvation will be found.

Living at the cross isn't a popular thought. It certainly wasn't among the people I hung out with in the '70s and '80s. Our misunderstanding of the concept mirrors much of the church still today. Back then I was in the

> **THE ADVENTURE (OF VICTORY OVER OUR EXALTED SOUL) INVOLVES FOLLOWING CHRIST TO THE CROSS EVERY SINGLE DAY.**

thick of what many called "the faith movement," part of the larger charismatic movement. If you wanted a pump-you-up, let's go, rah-rah message, that's where the action was. I don't say that dismissively; through this movement I really came into a love of the Word, into prayer, into an understanding that I can be an overcomer, and many other valuable things. I still appreciate the message of faith and victory.

But one of the things I noticed early on was how little talk about the cross there was. When it did happen, it was always something in the past tense—a past, onetime occurrence we appreciated. "Now we live at the victory of the resurrection" was the mindset. The cross was an already-paid price, the resurrection an ongoing reward. If you ever wanted to toss a wet blanket over those of us hyped up on raising our level of faith, all you had to do was mention "living at" or "bearing" the cross. The room would turn quiet. That somehow became an admission of defeat.

Maybe there was good reason for this. In the circles in which most of us grew up, "bearing my cross" or "carrying my cross" was code for "I'm a problem-plagued, defeated, suffering, joyless Christian right now." It meant being weighed down with burdens and inability to overcome predicaments. Christianity wasn't supposed to be much fun; believers weren't supposed to prosper but be "cross-bearers, suffering for Jesus."

In response, we did the oh-so-human thing: we threw out the baby and savored the bath water. We decided to forget bearing the cross and just experience resurrection power.

Our motive was good. Christ does invite us to embrace the abundant resurrection life. He does promise us more than we can ever imagine. And having faith in His promises is absolutely essential to receiving them.

ONLY THROUGH THE DAILY POWER OF THE CROSS DO WE PERPETUALLY RECEIVE THE POWER OF THE RESURRECTION.

But by the same token, moving on from the cross is a deadly mistake. Only through the daily power of the cross do we perpetually receive the power of the resurrection. Paul alludes to this in writing of his desire to "know [Christ] and the power of His resurrection and the fellowship of His sufferings, being conformed to His death; in order that I may attain to the resurrection from the dead" (Philippians 3:10–11).

Once again, this is a case of what seems to be near-absurd paradox-speak. Paul wants to share in the death of Christ just so he can be resurrected? What is this guy? Crazy? *Au contraire* . . . Paul had this whole "be in two places at the same time" thing down. He understood that through death comes life. To gain, we must lose. The crucifixion of our exalted *psuché* makes possible the release of power and life from our *pneuma*. Remember, the life of the spirit must be released through soul and body, not apart from them. Love is expressed through the soul, as is self-control and all other fruit of the spirit. Without a soul willing to submit to these forces of life, however, they can't be released.

Often you'll hear people say that Jesus went to the cross *so we wouldn't have to.* That is true only in a literal, physical sense. Preaching the cross this way, even though it's done with great appreciation for His sacrifice, borders on heresy. Jesus went to the cross so we *could* go there. His call to us is to *join* Him in His crucifixion—so that we may have life.

> [We are] always carrying about in the body the dying of Jesus, so that the life of Jesus also may be manifested in our body. For we who live are constantly being delivered over to death for Jesus' sake, so that the life of Jesus also may be manifested in our mortal flesh. (2 Corinthians 4:10–11)

Of course, Jesus' being crucified as our representative means we don't have to go through what He did physically. I'm not promoting self-punishment, flagellation, crawling over rocks until our hands and knees are shredded, living lives of misery and deprivation—just so we can identify with Christ's suffering. But where our soul is concerned, He took His *psuché* to the cross to make it possible for us to do the same. And this is the only way to daily identify with Him in the power of the resurrection: daily join Him at the cross. I realize that since this cannot be literal, you're probably wondering how this happens. We'll get there . . . tell your *psuché* to be patient.

You Lose, You Win

Throughout His ministry Christ was setting us up for this cross-resurrection paradox. Near the beginning He gave the Beatitudes, which revealed a kingdom of wealthy paupers, happy mourners, non-aggressive conquerors, quenched thirsty folks, self-enriching benefactors, realistic visionaries, militant pacifists, and winning losers (see Matthew 5:3–12). Later He told us the last will be first, and the first last (20:16); the least will be the greatest (Luke 9:48); the lowly and humble will be exalted (Matthew 23:12); and (one we're becoming familiar with), "He who has found his life will lose it, and he who has lost his life for My sake will find it" (10:39).

Quite simply, what enables us to understand these contradictory statements is realizing that we must deal with certain parts of ourselves differently. Once you're born again, what's in your spirit can be trusted, but much of what's still in your soul cannot. And the appetites of the flesh—your body—must also be controlled. If not, they'll crave extreme fulfillment, be it through sleep, food, sex, or the sating of any other natural appetite. Though it's a battle that must be waged, as the following story illustrates, the prize is worth the effort, no matter how long it takes.

> At the 1994 Winter Olympics in Norway, the name *Dan* took on a very special meaning. At his first Olympics in 1984, as an eighteen-year-old, speed skater Dan Jansen finished fourth in the 500 meters, beaten for a bronze medal by only sixteen-one-hundredths of a second, and he finished sixteenth in the 1,000.
>
> At his second Olympics in Calgary in 1988, on the morning he was to skate the 500 meters, he received a phone call from America. His twenty-seven-year-old sister, Jane, had been fighting leukemia for more than a year. She was dying. Dan spoke to her over the phone, but she was too sick to say anything in return. Their brother Mike relayed Jane's message: she wanted Dan to race for her. Before Dan skated that afternoon, however, he received the news that Jane had died. When he took

to the ice, perhaps he tried too hard for his sister. In the 500 meters, he slipped and fell in the first turn. He had never fallen before in a race. Four days later in the 1,000, he fell again, this time, of all places, in the straightaway.

At his third Olympics in 1992, he was expected to win the 500 meters, where he had already set world records. For four years he had been regarded as the best sprinter in the world. But he had trouble in the final turn and he finished fourth. In the 1,000 he tied for twenty-sixth.

At his fourth Olympics in 1994, Dan again was expected to win in the 500 meters, which was his specialty. Again tragedy struck. He didn't fall, but in the beginning of the final turn he fleetingly lost control of his left skate and put his hand down, slowing him just enough to finish in eighth place. Afterward, he apologized to his hometown of Milwaukee.

He had one race left, the 1,000 meter. One more race and then he would retire. At the midway point of the race, the clock showed he was skating at a world-record pace, and the crowd, including his wife and father, cheered. But with 200 meters to go, the hearts of the fans skipped a beat. Dan Jansen slipped. He didn't fall, but he slipped, touched his hand to the ice, regained control, and kept skating. When Dan crossed the finish line, he looked at the scoreboard and saw "WR" beside his name—world record. In his last race, Dan Jansen had finally won the gold medal.

Later that day as he stood on the award stand, Dan looked heavenward, acknowledging his late sister, Jane.

Jansen was asked to skate a victory lap. The lights were turned out, and a single spotlight illuminated Dan's last lap around the Olympic track, with a gold medal around his neck, roses in one arm, and his baby daughter—named Jane—in his other arm.

In the closing ceremony of the 1994 Olympics, Dan Jansen was chosen to carry the U.S. flag.

"Late in the afternoon of February 18, 1994," said writer Philip Hersh, "after Jansen had won the gold medal that eluded him in seven previous races over four Olympics and a decade, someone put a hand-lettered sign in the snow on the side of the main road from Lilleham- mer to Hamar. The sign said simply, 'Dan.' It spoke vol- umes about what the world thought about the man whose Olympic futility had finally ended in triumph."[2]

Dan Jansen's lone Olympic victory was made that much sweeter by repeated failure. His elation certainly meant more after suffering the agony of so many heartbreakers, as well as the tragedy he'd endured. In the same way, the sufferings we're sure to find in daily placing our soulish nature on the cross will pale in comparison to the resurrection life Christ extends to us. And just as Dan Jansen contin- ually longed for the day he'd finally claim an Olympic medal, we are moving toward the day when our soul will finally and completely yield to our spirit.

A Practical Picture

With all this talk of our soul dying, let's stop and clarify exactly what that means. Obviously we're not talking about a literal death, nor do we mean death to the soul's normal functions—our emotions, common sense, ability to reason, etc. Contrary to what some seem to believe, we don't stop thinking or squelch our feelings in some eso- teric attempt at spirituality. (God help us, haven't we already been through centuries of the church pretending to be "spiritual," a.k.a., having the emotional zeal of a doorknob?)

We're talking about death to the exalted life-force that came to the soul at the fall. This is what must remain at the cross. Then we can bring the functions of the soul—the God-given ability to think, reason, store information, emit emotion, and choose right courses of action—under the control or influence of the spirit (which indirectly brings them back under the Spirit's control).

Common sense is a God-given thing. He created our brains to instinctively know and figure things out. But under our own knowledge of good and evil, common sense turns into a prideful, arrogant display of our own wisdom and knowledge. It becomes a showcase for our natural, logical instincts. Under God's logic—His *logos*—common sense becomes a beautiful expression governed by His standards, His wisdom, and His truth applied to everyday life.

Likewise with anger (as an emotion). In itself, there's nothing wrong with anger; God intentionally incorporated it into the spectrum of our emotions. And obviously Jesus displayed it (e.g., Mark 11:15–17). Unfortunately, many interpret this as an excuse for their own uncontrolled anger. Let me assure you that without this emotion being under the spirit's control, it is sinful. Jesus' outburst was completely holy because His anger was under the control of His spirit. He, a perfect, unfallen human, never once had uncontrolled anger that was rooted in His *psuché*. He controlled the soul's reaction and yielded to the Holy Spirit's control. That is what it means to be a *pneumatikos*.

To follow Christ's example, every natural element of our soul must be influenced by the life in our spirit. When this is happening, we'll say no to our instinctive desire for self-promotion and vindication. We will turn the other cheek while our *psuché* is screaming to punch the lights out of

> **TO FOLLOW CHRIST'S EXAMPLE, EVERY NATURAL ELEMENT OF OUR SOUL MUST BE INFLUENCED BY THE LIFE IN OUR SPIRIT.**

the guy who just insulted us. The integrity in our spirit will cause us to be truthful on our taxes when we know we could easily get away with exaggerating a few write-offs here and there.

Walking according to our spirit will mean being free enough that we can submit ourselves to a loss of freedom for the sake of not causing another believer to stumble. Paul vowed that he wouldn't let any of his personal liberties become so important that they might hinder a brother's walk with the Lord (1 Corinthians 8:9–13). That is a crucified *psuché*!

The apostle also discovered that it's better to boast in imperfections and failures if we're going to boast at all. He knew the upsidedown kingdom principle: "Power is perfected in weakness" (2 Corinthians 12:9). Is this some kind of "turn lemons into lemonade" optimism? Not at all. Paul had learned that recognizing and acknowledging the inherent weaknesses of his soul and flesh reminded and forced him to rely on God's ability in his spirit. Even in deprivation and persecution for the cause of Christ, Paul somehow was able to draw on God's power in his spirit and silence the self-preservation instincts of his soul as well as the body's desire for comfort (11:22–12:6).

Now, that's a *pneumatikos*!

Where the Rubber Meets the Road

Sounds wonderful on paper, doesn't it? It's a different story when we have to walk this out in everyday life—especially in a fallen world that doesn't give a rip about keeping its *psuché* on the cross. (If it even knows or cares that it has a *psuché*.) In addition, it's tough to get excited about the challenge of wielding control over your soul if it's been controlled an unwanted, unyielding stronghold.

What about those mentioned earlier who've been damaged or

scarred by others' actions upon them, those now controlled by a truth based not on reality but on their interpretation of reality? How does taking their *psuché* to the cross have anything to do with healing, restoration, and freedom? Weren't they the victims?

The truth is, God is not blind to those struggling with strongholds or those with a tarnished soul as a result of someone else's sins. And neither have I ignored those individuals in our discussion of *psuché*'s death. Grace, mercy, compassion, love, kindness . . . these are the elements God promises to lavish on His children, especially those who are wounded.

Yet taking *psuché* to the cross is not a requirement based on life's particulars. God doesn't handpick those who must lay down their soul based upon what good or bad has happened. The soul's exaltation is a universal problem that began with the original man, Adam; it's a state-of-the-union issue, not a case-by-case ruling. Enthroned *psuché* is what Christ came to depose. In order to live in the victory He's already provided, we must die to what's clinging to its lofty seat.

> **THE SOUL'S EXALTATION IS A UNIVERSAL PROBLEM THAT BEGAN WITH THE ORIGINAL MAN, ADAM; IT'S A STATE-OF-THE-UNION ISSUE, NOT A CASE-BY-CASE RULING.**

Seems a bit inverted, doesn't it? Yet as Christians we're called to live a paradoxical existence in a backward world. We follow a truth that doesn't make sense to our natural souls, and we deny the very things this world is after most. The great preacher-teacher A. W. Tozer put it this way:

> A real Christian is an odd number, anyway. He feels supreme love for One whom he has never seen; talks

familiarly every day to Someone he cannot see; expects to go to heaven on the virtue of Another; empties himself in order to be full; admits he is wrong so he can be declared right; goes down in order to get up; is strongest when he is weakest, richest when he is poorest and happiest when he feels the worst. He dies so he can live; forsakes in order to have; gives away so he can keep; sees the invisible; hears the inaudible; and knows that which passeth knowledge.[3]

Amen, and then some! We're a strange, funny bunch, aren't we? And yet we follow a wonderfully peculiar Savior who's determined to turn things right-side-up. He understands that the moment new birth takes place, our *zoé*-filled spirit wants to express itself—to "get out," to fly! It wants to commune with God the way it was originally made to, served by the soul and the body.

But, again, that spirit is stuck behind a still-exalted soul bent on getting its own way. It's trapped behind thick walls fortified by pain, sadness, and suffering. To be released, this healing, rejuvenating spirit must go through the soul—the mind, the emotions, and the will—making our soul the release valve. It can shut the spirit down in a matter of seconds. (We experience this every time we ignore that gentle nudging of the Holy Spirit inside us.) So while the spirit wants to soar, the soul is perfectly content to restrict the spirit by staying grounded and in control.

Thankfully, our Maker understands this struggle completely. He wants to aid us, not condemn us, in our process of transformation. And He is patient, knowing we can't change the soul instantly. So He goes to work on it, usually one area at a time. He doesn't hand us a list of ten things He wants us to change by next week. Instead, the Spirit usually spotlights one or two problem areas—we call that conviction—and deals with us until we have that area of the soul under control, living at the cross.

Romans 5:10 says,

> If while we were enemies we were reconciled to God through the death of His Son, much more, having been reconciled, we shall be saved by His life.

His life. *Zoé.* Our salvation, our transformation from walking according to soul life to spirit life. The same seed that planted the life-changing *logos* in our spirit is ever expanding its roots in our soul—one day at a time, one issue at a time.

And believe it or not, you'll get there. You're gradually establishing a dual residency at both the cross and the resurrection—laying down your life to roll away your stone. With the Spirit's help, you're becoming a *pneumatikos.* You're becoming who you are!

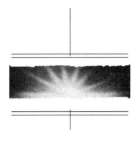

CHAPTER 10

You Deserve a Break Today

I've been busy before. *Really* busy. You've undoubtedly been there also. But I hope you've never gone to the hectic extremes I did during one not-too-distant season of my life. Allow me to explain.

From 2003 to 2004, my good friend Chuck Pierce and I embarked on a prayer tour of all fifty states in a year. This wasn't a series of on-offs in which we flew into town, muttered a few prayers, and left that night or the following morning. God had challenged us with specific assignments for each state, which meant that more often than not we would be at multiple sites in a state throughout the week, conducting services, leading prayer gatherings, teaching, making prophetic declarations, serving the local bodies . . . an assortment that required much energy (as did the grueling travel).

Meanwhile, I was still serving as pastor of our church body in Colorado Springs, and would fly back every Sunday to preach and minister there. As any pastor can tell you, pastoring demands more than your average eight-to-five job. Combine those daily responsibilities and my travel schedule with the calling God was increasing in my life to intercede for our nation's government and leaders—a calling that frequently entailed strategic trips to Washington, D.C. After a single year, I'd made more than seventy out-of-state trips—an average of almost one and a half per week.

In the midst of all this, I was also writing books, mentoring leaders, launching nationwide prayer networks, meeting the needs of my family—which were more emotional than anything else, given my frequent absence—and, of course, making sure my time with the Lord wasn't getting elbowed out.

When it was all said and done, I was spent. Literally spent. Doctors discovered that my adrenals were partially burnt out and that I was existing on a next-to-nothing energy supply. I would sleep for ten or more hours and still wake up over-fatigued. Often it would take me most of the morning for my mind to shake off the grogginess and begin functioning normally. To restore my adrenal levels, I took a prescribed combination of vitamins and supplements, in addition to exercising and, naturally, resting. Not an overnight remedy—I needed an extended break from life.

There's rarely a time when any of us wouldn't like a break, no matter how extensive. We live at a breakneck speed that stops only temporarily during the few moments our phones, PDAs, or laptops are off. It doesn't help that whatever free time remains is usually filled with more noise (TV, iPod, the list continues). With our pace, it's become a necessity to take some time off every now and then.

Yet there's a big difference in wanting a vacation from everyday life and needing soul-rest. As we've learned, ever since the fall our *psuché* has been in a state of chaos. Because of our decision to elevate our own knowledge over God's, we have lacked the inherent peace with which He originally made our soul to exist. In other words, for thousands of years now we've been in distress rather than His rest.

Christ came to change all that by taking *psuché* to the cross, where

He becomes its Lord again. The result, as we'll see, is soul-rest. In Matthew 11:28, Jesus says, "Come to Me, all who are weary and heavy-laden, and I will give you rest." Safe to say we all qualify for this "maxed-out" club. And if we come to our Messiah, He promises rest. A respite. A break. A much-needed breather.

MORE CRAZY TALK?

Once again, however, Jesus couches His offer in paradoxical terms. Want rest? Good, then "take My yoke upon you and learn from Me, for I am gentle and humble in heart, and you will find rest for your souls. For My yoke is easy and My burden is light" (v. 29–30).

It's another of those "huh?" moments. A yoke is a hard, wooden crosspiece draped around the neck of an ox or horse and used to plow a field. It puts the animal pulling it in total submission to a master's direction (the spiritual correlation is blatant). A yoke is anything *but* light, easy, or freeing—it's cumbersome, annoying, and distressing. And Jesus offers us the vacation of a lifetime for our souls . . . if we'll only put on one of these "wonderful, nonrestrictive" contraptions? There He goes again!

There's a word in His statement, however, that illuminates the entire offer. *Chréstos.* Virtually every version renders this as "easy," and translators certainly aren't wrong for doing so. But because of the limitations of this English word, we're missing out on the deeper meaning. Let me explain.

Imagine you're a construction worker contracted to build a giant new bank downtown. According to the blueprints, this building will dwarf all others around it. Your assignment for the next few weeks is to frame the structure with steel I beams—a key task that must be done without error. Today your foreman has instructed you to secure the massive bolts on those beams. One problem, though: He hasn't given you any tools. Apparently you're expected to tighten the connective bolts using only your hands.

Sounds ludicrous. If the public knew that's how the I beams were fastened, by hand, no one would set foot in this grandiose edifice. In fact, the whole place would probably collapse before you reached the next phase of construction. What was needed for the task was the right tool—a large adjustable wrench or, in most cases, a machine built specifically for tightening and securing the bolts. With one of those you could successfully accomplish the assignment because you'd have what was necessary.

> **OUR SOUL NEEDS AN ADJUSTMENT THAT ONLY JESUS CAN PROVIDE, AND IT COMES THROUGH BEARING HIS YOKE.**

When Jesus describes His yoke as "easy" (*chréstos*), He is saying it is that which is necessary. The root word, *chraomai*, means "to furnish what is needed."[1] "Easy" defines this term because that which is difficult becomes easy when one is given what is necessary or needed. In this verse, what is His yoke necessary for? *Psuché*-rest. Our soul requires a special tool to be loosened and given rest. Our soul needs an adjustment that only Jesus can provide, and it comes through bearing His yoke.

Interestingly enough, the word for "taking" this yoke upon us is *airô*, which, as we saw earlier, means "exalt." It's the same word Jesus used in instructing us to "take up" our cross (Matthew 16:24–26). Once again our choice is obvious: either exalt our *psuché* or choose to lift up Jesus' lordship, take His yoke, and proclaim death upon our soulish nature. Either cling to the sinful yoke of our Adamic nature or bear the ultimately freeing yoke He offers.

You Can Learn a Lot From an Ox

Even after acknowledging the situation on these terms, it's astounding how many people still want to follow their own scheme.

Like the arrogant ship captain, we'll do anything to prove our way is better than God's:

> The captain looked into the dark night and saw faint lights in the distance. Immediately he told his signalman to send a message: "Alter your course 10 degrees south."
>
> Promptly a return message was received: "Alter your course 10 degrees north."
>
> The captain was angered; his command had been ignored. So he sent a second message: "Alter your course 10 degrees south—I am the captain!"
>
> Soon another message was received: "Alter your course 10 degrees north—I am seaman third class Jones."
>
> Immediately the captain sent a third message, knowing the fear it would evoke: "Alter your course 10 degrees south—I am a battleship."
>
> Then the reply came: "Alter your course 10 degrees north—I am a lighthouse."[2]

Stubbornness comes in countless prideful forms. It seems we'd rather do anything but concede our self-proclaimed position as top dog. As a result, we try to define our own way of finding rest for our soul via money, fame, success, sex, religion, or various other man-made solutions. We remain stiff-necked, which in fact, is a term that originated from the concept of being yoked. The Hebrew word *qasheh* gave the literal description for an ox that refused to pull the plow.[3] With a heavy, restrictive structure on its neck and a farmer pulling it in various directions, an ox would sometimes rebel and fight the yoke by stiffening its neck.

The Old Testament mentions this term on several occasions (e.g., Deuteronomy 10:16; 31:27; Psalm 75:5), yet it's in Jeremiah 17:23 where we find a perfect take on those who refuse the rest that Christ offers: "Yet they did not listen or incline their ears, but stiffened their necks in order not to listen or take correction."

That would be *psuché*.

I see people react like this all the time. Say one thing from the pulpit that crosses *psuché*—pun intended—and you'll notice that certain folks literally stiffen up. Talk about tithing one too many times. Mention forgiving past offenders just a little too often. Have the music too loud, the sermon too long, or the prayers too passionate. You've rattled some theological cages and crossed their "church" boundaries, and you can be sure they're going to let you know.

I've been in situations where I thought that as a spiritual leader I needed to step in and prayerfully say something about the way someone was treating his wife or children. Some, rather than receiving my words as nudges from the Lord, have responded with a "how dare you" look. Why? Because I offended their *psuché*, which made them even more stiff-necked. They wouldn't take the yoke. By its nature, no *psuché* likes to be held in check, corrected, or rebuked. And so it does the logical thing (by man's logic, that is): whines, pouts, kicks, screams, throws a tantrum, gives the "silent treatment," takes it up with the board of elders, stops tithing, leaves the church altogether . . . you get my point. The soul gets squirmy when its turf is trodden upon.

Would You Please Stop Crying?!

We have a choice not to respond this way. There's an alternative that leads to true rest rather than ruffled feathers. Whether you feel like it or not, you *can* yield to the direction in which your soul's true master, Jesus, is pulling. He wants your soul to be at rest. He wants it to be, as Psalm 131 says, "like a weaned child."

Read how David brought such rest to his soul:

O Lord, my heart is not proud, nor my eyes haughty;

nor do I involve myself in great matters, or in things too
difficult for me.

Surely I have composed and quieted my soul;

like a weaned child rests against his mother,

My soul is like a weaned child within me. (vv. 1–2)

David contrasts an arrogant soul that takes on assignments beyond its true ability to one that is weaned, quiet, and restful.

We are weaned from something when we've reached a certain level of maturity. The Hebrew word for weaned, *gamal*, actually means "ripe" and refers to when a fruit is ready to be plucked from the branch.[4] At that point, it's ready to move on and serve its purpose. Likewise, a weaned child is one who doesn't need her mother's milk anymore. Contrast with an unweaned child, screaming to be fed by Mama when Mama isn't available. The former is composed and quiet; the latter is uncontrolled and demanding.

I'll never forget the first time Ceci left me alone with our first-born, Sarah, who was being breastfed at the time.

"Don't worry, sweetie. I'll be back in time to feed her," Ceci said. Nothing to worry about, right?

Wrong. I can't remember if Ceci was late returning or if Sarah's timing was a little off, but the reason didn't matter once my precious four-month-old woke up and realized she was hungry. In fact, judging by the way she cried, she was *way* beyond famished. I mean, if she didn't get a meal within the next two minutes, she was surely going to die. (Isn't this how all babies think?)

I tried reasoning: "Baby Girl, I'm sorry, I don't have what Mommy has . . . but she's on her way home right now if you'll hold on just a bit." Didn't work.

I tried faking her out by continuously putting a pacifier in her mouth and holding her close as she would be if she were eating. Not a chance.

And, of course, as any dad has done, I tried the old rock-her-till-she's-too-dizzy-to-cry move. *I* ended up nauseated.

After what seemed like hours, Ceci walked in. Within two seconds after she began to feed, Sarah was as content as a . . . well, as a suckling baby.

Several months later, home alone with my weaned daughter, it was a night-and-day difference. When Sarah became hungry, rather than a nuclear meltdown deserving of Oscar recognition, she ate from another source, and Mama came home to a peaceful dad and child.

WE CAN KEEP *PSUCHÉ* UNDER CONTROL BY BRINGING IT TO THE CROSS AND TAKING ON THE YOKE OF JESUS.

We can react either way to Christ's offer of rest: whine, cry, and scream about wanting our way, or settle down, take His yoke, and know that He'll come through with His promise. We can listen to rampaging *psuché*'s "I want what I want, and I want it *now*!!! I don't care what anyone else thinks, I've been wronged! I deserve this! I'm going to get my way, no matter what You say, God!" Or we can keep *psuché* under control by bringing it to the cross and taking on the yoke of Jesus. Only the latter yields a rested, ripened, matured, and weaned soul that trusts its Lord completely. All else leads to discontent.

FREE TO GROW

Let's take a look at some biblical examples of souls that took the way to the Lord's rest. We've already highlighted David's writing in Psalm 131, and he makes statements elsewhere worth noting in regard to soul-contentment. In 116:7, he writes,

Return to your rest, O my soul, for the Lord has dealt
bountifully with you.

"Dealt bountifully" is the same Hebrew word translated "wean" in
Psalm 131—*gamal.*[5] Here again it evokes the word picture of ripened
fruit. When you have "dealt bountifully" with a fruit, you've nourished
its source with everything needed. You've done all you can to feed it
properly; as a result, it will ripen and mature. The analogy remains
true with a small child. If you feed him the way he needs to be fed, he
will grow and mature to where he no longer relies solely on milk but
also desires solid food. He is rested in his maturity. In this verse, the
process brings rest to our soul.

In 142:7, David says,

Bring my soul out of prison, so that I may give thanks to
Your name;
the righteous will surround me, for You will deal bountifully with me.

Again, *gamal* shows the Lord's faithful provision that leads to a matur-
ing of the soul. Yet notice what David also says in the first part:
"Bring my soul out of prison." *Get my* psuché *out of jail!*

Jesus went to the depths of hell to free our *psuché* from the dun-
geon of our sinfulness. Without salvation, our soul is destined for a
shackled, confined future; with it, it's bound for the freedom it was
always intended to enjoy.

Charles Simpson, in *Pastoral Renewal,* writes:

I met a young man not long ago who dives for exotic fish
for aquariums. He said one of the most popular aquarium
fish is the shark. He explained that if you catch a small
shark and confine it, it will stay a size proportionate to

the aquarium. Sharks can be six inches long yet fully matured. But if you turn them loose in the ocean, they grow to their normal length of eight feet.[6]

The *psuché*, confined in the prison of our old nature, will never be able to experience the growth, maturity, and ultimately the rest Christ offers. However, when we take His yoke and allow Him to establish true rest and freedom within us, our soul can develop to God's intended, bountiful growth.

YOU CALLING ME A DUMB SHEEP?

Consider the beginning of David's most well-known passage, Psalm 23:

> The Lord is my shepherd,
>   I shall not want.
> He makes me lie down in green pastures;
>   He leads me beside quiet waters.
> He restores my soul;
>   He guides me in the paths of righteousness
> For His name's sake. (vv. 1–3)

The one sentence can be translated literally: "He leads me beside the waters of rest." How? The very next statement explains: By restoring our soul. Restoring is the word *shuwb*, which means "movement back to the point of departure."[7]

Restoring our soul, returning it to the point of departure, requires what Jesus spoke about in Matthew 11:28–30: the Lord's yoke, His shepherdship, as pictured in this psalm. We see this imagery through verses such as Isaiah 53:6 ("All of us like sheep have gone astray, each of us has turned to his own way") and 1 Peter 2:25 ("You were continually straying like sheep, but now you have returned to the Shepherd and Guardian of your souls").

At the fall, through Adam, we all came out from under the Lord's shepherdship. We went our own way, deciding to exalt our own soul, our own knowledge, above our Master. *Thank You very much, God, but I'll take it from here. I know You made all this around me and You know the most intricate parts of me, but I'll tell You what: I think I can do better. I'll be my own lord, I'll run my own life, if You don't mind.* And ever since then we've been running around like aimless sheep, trying to find peace for our soul.

David's solution—and one we'd all do well to embrace—is to return to the point of departure. Return to the place where our soul wandered off like a lost, dumb sheep. Where is that? It's at the lordship of Jesus. We all renounced

> **TO FIND OUR WAY BACK INTO HIS PROMISE OF REST AND RESTORATION, WE MUST RETURN TO THE PLACE OF FULLY ACKNOWLEDGING HIM AS MASTER.**

God's authority when we deferred to our sinful nature. To find our way back into His promise of rest *and* restoration, we must return to the place of fully acknowledging Him as Master. And that exact place is found at—you guessed it—the cross of Christ.

It's not just coincidence that Psalm 23, a picture of a restored soul, follows Psalm 22, a picture of the cross. Three of the seven sayings of Christ on the cross, He took from this psalm. "My God, my God, why have You forsaken me?" (v. 1) is how it begins. The message is clear: We must go through the cross (Psalm 22) to find rest for our soul (Psalm 23). We must take His yoke to find everlasting freedom.

ENTER INTO MY REST, SON

I know of a man who's found such permanent freedom even though he spends his days in a prison cell. He's serving a 365-year sentence and will never have a shot at parole. He regularly receives death threats. Mention his name and blood begins to boil. In fact, it's hard to even think of his name without visions of murder and demonic activity.

To America, he is known as the Son of Sam.

To God, he's simply known as "son."

Few lives exude the transforming power of Jesus to bring a soul into true rest and freedom more than that of David Berkowitz. As a child, he created a whirlwind of destruction wherever he went. Though adopted by a Jewish couple and raised in a loving home, he continually felt tormented by a dark, outside force. Often he'd have seizures or begin screaming and running around wildly for no apparent reason. His teenage years were filled with fights, bouts of depression, and ongoing thoughts of suicide. At times, his body would shake as he felt compelled to throw himself in front of a moving bus or subway. After losing his mother to cancer when he was fourteen, the turmoil only escalated.

David graduated from high school in the early 1970s and immediately served in the army for three years. After returning to New York City, he met a group of guys involved in the occult. He already felt his life had been one attempted escape from a satanic force trying to get at him, so after delving more into this darkness he decided to yield to the devil's pulls. During the following years he studiously read Anton LaVey's *Satanic Bible* and began engaging in rituals such as animal sacrifices.

Then came the summer of 1976. On the evening of July 29, David executed the first of a series of murders that would continue for more than a year and eventually capture the attention—and fear—of the whole city. By the time he was arrested and sent to prison, he'd achieved legendary status as a mass-murderer.

But even there, David's torment continued. His depression, erratic behavior, and suicide attempts earned him the nickname "Berserkow-itz" and caused supervisors to send him to a psychiatric hospital. At one point, another prisoner slashed his neck open, barely missing a vein that would have surely drained him of life.

Ten years into his sentencing, David met a fellow inmate who shared the gospel with him. He couldn't fathom a God who would be interested in a notorious killer and, naturally, shunned the man. But after the two slowly developed a relationship, David became more interested in this possible hope offered from heaven. After reading Psalm 34:6 ("This poor man cried, and the Lord heard him and saved him out of all his troubles") one night while alone in his cell, his heart was captured.

"When I got up [from praying] it felt as if a very heavy but invis-ible chain that had been around me for so many years was broken," David says. "A peace flooded over me. I did not understand what was happening. But in my heart I just knew that my life, somehow, was going to be different."[8]

And it was. The man responsible for so much destruction, who'd both endured and inflicted so much torture, now felt at rest for the first time in his life. His soul was finally free.

Not many of us have stories to match David Berkowitz's. Yet whether we've killed, stolen, lied, or simply lusted in our heart, sin is sin. And *psuché* is *psuché*. We're all in the same boat, thanks to our fallen nature, and we're all in need of soul-rest. Even after being saved, Berkowitz faced an uphill daily battle—still does, to this day. His past tries to haunt him, just like ours does. Our soul loves to bring up old conditions, habits, and mindsets.

I won't lie—it's not easy to change. Our *psuché* is a raging beast that's been pampered in the wild for thousands of years. Every time we've sinned against God and exalted our desires above His, we've fed this soulish animal.

Yet Christ offers us all the same rest from this fallen *psuché*. "Take My yoke upon you," He says paradoxically, "and you will find rest for your souls." *Nothing but glorious.* For when we place the uncomfortable, ultra-restrictive yoke on our fallen soul, when we place *psuché* at the cross and recognize our Savior's lordship, transformation begins. Not just minor renovation, but lasting, permanent change that molds us more into the image of Jesus, whom we were meant to look like in the first place.

The same God who brought a satanic, demon-possessed killer to the cross can certainly silence our raging soul and usher in His rest.

PART III

THE PROCESS

CHAPTER 11

THIS MEANS WAR!

The good, devout man first makes inner preparation for the actions he has later to perform. His outward actions do not draw him into lust and vice; rather it is he who bends them into the shape of reason and right judgment. Who has a stiffer battle to fight than the man who is striving to conquer himself?—Thomas à Kempis[1]

My friend George is a phenomenal father, an outstanding entrepreneur, and a wonderful man. He is not, however, a very good fix-it guy.

When it comes to repairs around the house, George apparently is intent on having his wife and kids master the whole "patience is a virtue" thing. When there's a broken toilet, a busted doorknob, or anything else that goes bump, creak, and squeak in the night, George would rather cross the Sahara barefoot than call in a qualified repairman. He figures he'll spend his money on better things than paying someone to take apart his own stove, air-conditioner, commode, or car.

Notice I didn't exactly say he *fixed* those things. Yep, George is a master of disassembly. He can take apart a faulty refrigerator faster than a hot grill melts an ice cube. Putting it—or anything else—back together in working order . . . that's another issue.

Gotta love a guy who tries, right?

In a way, we're at the same place in this book. Ten chapters ago, we established that we're broken and in need of the ultimate fix-it job. In that same span, we've disassembled the makeup of our being. We've evaluated various aspects of the soul and discussed our need to go by the Owner's Manual, to return to the way God created us. (Aren't you glad He didn't void the warranty?!) We've learned that, thanks to Jesus' provision on the cross, our spirit is already redeemed once we make Him Lord of our life. Our soul, meanwhile, is in the process of being redeemed.

That's all well and good. It's valuable knowledge that can definitely help each of us on our journey toward redemption. But if we stopped, we'd be no better off than George's family is every time he deconstructs another household fixture. If this book simply helped you accumulate more head knowledge, then I've failed as a writer. What we need is something that moves us to action. Transforming action. Life-altering action that takes us closer than ever to becoming the people we're supposed to be!

Calling All Soldiers

I live in a military town that houses no fewer than five bases. It's virtually impossible for me to go anywhere locally without seeing soldiers in uniform. Throughout the year, especially during times of war, it's heartbreaking to watch these servicemen and servicewomen leave their families as they head overseas. Yet to a soldier, each is willing to go for one reason: freedom.

They fight for their own. They fight for America's. They fight for that of other nations and, more specifically, for that of the citizens of those countries. Many times, for freedom, they fight an unseen enemy, an adversary content only to be seen in the destruction and terror it leaves in its wake.

These brave people are willing to put their lives on the line for the sake of freedom. But can you imagine if their commanding officers had no strategy for the fight? What if those in charge knew nothing about the enemy? What if, upon arriving, these soldiers were told it was every man for himself? "Thanks for coming guys; now you're on your own. Good luck with everything."

Obviously this would never happen in a war. And neither should it happen in your life. By now, we're well aware that we're in a fight for our soul's redemption. We will either choose to defend the *psuché* or we'll fight to become spirit-guided beings. There is no middle ground.

In addition, we cannot assume that participating in the battle is good enough. We must have a strategy. We must have a call to action.

If a front-line soldier plows haphazardly into the open, he'll almost certainly lose his life. Wisely, he waits for a commander to muster the troops, articulate a plan, and make a call to action. (War isn't always fought like this today, but the principles still apply.)

The following chapters are your command to *charge!* They're the practical tactics of warfare that you can execute on the battlefield against your soulish nature. Without them you lack strategy to win this fight. With them you can surely conquer your self-pleasing enemy.

Five Steps

At the outset, I mentioned Jesus' promise of making those whom He sets free "free *indeed.*" Let's take another look at that passage as we establish five essential tactics for gaining freedom:

> As He spoke these things, many came to believe in Him.
> So Jesus was saying to those Jews who had believed Him,

"If you abide in My word, then you are truly disciples of Mine; and you will know the truth, and the truth will make you free."

They answered Him, "We are Abraham's descendants and have never yet been enslaved to anyone; how is it that You say, 'You will become free'?"

Jesus answered them, "Truly, truly, I say to you, everyone who commits sin is the slave of sin. The slave does not remain in the house forever; the son does remain forever. So if the Son makes you free, you will be free indeed. I know that you are Abraham's descendants; yet you seek to kill Me, because My word has no place in you. I speak the things which I have seen with My Father; therefore you also do the things which you heard from your father" (John 8:30–38).

Within this single section lie five distinct steps on freedom's road. We'll spend the remainder of this book delving deeper into each, but for now, here they are in order:

(1) believe
(2) abide in his word
(3) know the truth
(4) be free
(5) be free indeed

Before launching, let me re-remind you: This is not simply a five-step contract to wholeness. I don't plan on offering quick fixes, because our soul's journey is not a quick *anything*. This is a process. *Life* is a process! I have organized these points into a structure, but don't think that by zipping through and checking off a to-do list you'll automatically arrive at the destination for which you were created. Obviously, God desires that you become who you were meant to be.

But 99.9 percent of the time, His will involves *molding* you into His Son's image *through* each step of the way. In other words, there's no such thing as fast-forwarding or TiVo-ing your way to soul freedom. God's a big fan of doing things in real time.

Believe: IT'S MORE THAN JUST A HALLMARK WORD

Jesus had just finished declaring Himself as the Son of God to a skeptical Jewish crowd. He had not only told them, "You are from below, I am from above" (John 8:23), He'd also noted that nothing He did was out of His own *psuché*. He only did what He saw His Father doing (vv. 28–29). Christ was the ultimate *pneumatikos*.

Imagine if a close friend came up and said this to you today. As much as you loved him, your soulish nature would indignantly inflate. *Who does he think he is, saying I'm from "below"? He's got some nerve to come in here and talk about being all perfect and higher than me.* Like a blowfish, *psuché*

> GOD DESIRES THAT YOU BECOME WHO YOU WERE MEANT TO BE. BUT 99.9 PERCENT OF THE TIME, HIS WILL INVOLVES MOLDING YOU INTO HIS SON'S IMAGE THROUGH EACH STEP OF THE WAY.

naturally swells when there's even a hint of danger—which, to the soul, means someone putting it in its place.

And yet how did many of the people hearing Jesus' words respond? They *believed* in Him. I liken this to the born-again experience. John 1:12 says, "As many as received Him, to them He gave the right to become children of God, even to those who believe in His name." We can't even begin to believe the truth of Jesus Christ if we remain completely in the soul's realm. It takes the invasion of the Holy Spirit—revelation—for us to take in the reality of Jesus. When this occurs, we are born again.

At that point, we receive the very nature of God. His blueprint and schematic are in our spirit, which is now in complete union with Him. Here, we lack nothing as we become a mirror image of Christ Himself. Paul states it this way: "In Him all the fullness of Deity dwells in bodily form, and in Him you have been made complete, and He is the head over all rule and authority" (Colossians 2:9–10). Being in Christ also means that all His promises and provisions are legally ours.

> **WE ARE IN THE PROCESS OF BEING TRANSFORMED—BECOMING OUTWARDLY WHO WE ALREADY ARE INWARDLY.**

But as we've also learned, that's only the beginning of our transformation. We are in the *process* of being transformed—becoming outwardly who we already are inwardly. The salvation of our spirit serves as the gateway for our complete spiritual redemption, opening the way to a complete and eternal salvation of our entire being.

As in Times of Old

There's possibly no better example of this initial step of believing and entering a process of salvation than Israel's journey out of Egypt during Old Testament times. Highlighting portions of their story will serve to remind us of some of the important things we've covered.

We all know the Jewish exodus from Egypt as a powerful account of God's miraculous provision to save His chosen people (Exodus 7–18). But it's also a picture of His miraculous deliverance of us today.

Just as the Israelites sacrificed a perfect lamb and put its blood on their doorposts and mantles during the first Passover, we are cleansed by the lifeblood of the ultimate Passover lamb, Jesus, at salvation (John 1:29).

The analogy continues: Even after leaving Egypt, the Israelites faced a crossroads once they came to the Red Sea. As they crossed with massive walls of water on both sides, they were essentially being baptized into a new life. Their past life in Egypt was being left behind and would eventually be swept away, just as their Egyptian pursuers were when the Lord closed the waters back again. In the same way, the symbolic act of baptism pictures our old nature and the sins of our past being washed away. Rising from the water, it depicts our emergence as a new creation being resurrected from spiritual death to spiritual life.

Despite all the spectacular events of Israel's exodus, however, it still took more than forty years for this chosen nation to get to where the Lord had promised. What caused the delay? The answer has become cliché: They were out of Egypt, but Egypt wasn't out of them. Idolatry, fear, murmuring, rebellion, unbelief—all soulish symptoms of their rebellious and wounded hearts. Indeed, the Lord had to work on their souls—*continuously*—before they could possess the earthly fruits of His promise.

When they finally did receive their inheritance, they experienced a reality that's still real for us today: that which belonged to Israel as a legal inheritance had to be possessed militarily. It would not automatically fall into their laps just because God had said it was theirs. The *legal* needed to become the *experiential.* Information needed to become revelation. What had already taken place in the spirit needed to be worked out in the natural.

Sound familiar? What Christ has given us legally as an inheritance—we are heirs of God and fellow heirs with Christ (Romans

8:17)—will not automatically fall into our laps either. Imagine how frustrating it was for the Israelites to have been miraculously rescued by God and handpicked as the hope for His will, only to find the way blocked by seemingly insurmountable obstacles . . . and then wander in the desert for decades. By the same token, how frustrating is it when God promises us something great, yet twenty years later we find ourselves still waiting for the fulfillment to come about? We beat on the stone from the inside, wondering when the grave of unfulfilled promises will yield to the promised resurrection.

Here we are again, then: *If I am, why don't I?* All of us have discovered at some point that our promised inheritance in Christ isn't necessarily what we're possessing. Like Israel, we're not enjoying all the fruits He promised us. There's a dichotomy that seems to rule the day.

Pause and think about the correlation for a moment. Before they could possess the land, the Israelites had to overcome various giants standing in the way. Likewise, you have giants that try to keep you from possessing your inheritance. Theirs were physical; most of yours are in your *psuché.* Have they become so strong that you've wanted to go back to your Egypt, as the Israelites did? Even after seeing the land they were to inherit, many gave up hope, resigning to the notion that there was no way they could conquer. *Psuché* doesn't like to face giants. Have you given up hope for your inheritance because the barriers loom too large? Please don't!

God is for you, just as He was for Israel. He encouraged them:

> Every place on which the sole of your foot treads, I have
> given it to you, just as I spoke to Moses. . . . No man will
> be able to stand before you all the days of your life. Just
> as I have been with Moses, I will be with you; I will not
> fail you or forsake you. (Joshua 1:3, 5)

He is saying the same to you.

THE CONQUERORS TREAD

When God told Israel He would give them every place where they stepped (v. 3), He wasn't saying they would simply waltz into their Promised Land unopposed. Far from it. The term He used for "tread" in Hebrew is *darak*, a warfare term, not a leisurely stroll marking out an inheritance.[2] This was a conqueror's tread, a war march. The word originated from the concept of treading the grapes in a winepress. Each step expressed the fruit's juice. This eventually became the same word used during war when a bow was bent back to shoot an arrow. Even today in Israel, *darak* is used by commanding officers when giving the order for soldiers to load their weapons. Obviously, it's not a passive concept.

So when the Lord told Joshua He would give the Israelites every place upon which they set their feet, He was being not only their savior but their general. *If you have your weapons loaded, your bows drawn back, and you're willing to tread through this territory as only a conqueror can . . . then you can possess what I'm giving.*

Are your weapons loaded for your fight against *psuché*? Have you declared war, and are you in the warrior's position, with arrows pointed straight at the enemy? Or are you passively waiting, hoping things work out, that maybe someday you'll change for good? And if they don't, well, maybe it just wasn't meant to be. Perhaps it wasn't in God's will or timing, right?

Wrong.

You will have to war for your promised freedom. "But in all these things we overwhelmingly conquer through Him who loved us" (Romans 8:37). You can win!

TAKE YOUR INHERITANCE

The warfare terms continue in the first chapter of Joshua when Israel's commanding officer rallied his leaders by instructing them to "pass through the midst of the camp and command the people, saying, 'Prepare provisions for yourselves, for within three days you are to cross this Jordan, to go in to possess the land which the Lord your God is giving you, to possess it'" (v. 11). Both uses of *possess* are translated from *yarash*, which has two related but different meanings. First, it defines a legal heir, someone who by law inherits property. Second, it means a military invasion in order to seize and settle in the land.[3] Easy to see that the dual meaning creates an interesting scenario in which there's both action and reaction, cause and effect.

So does God give us the land, or do we take it?

Yes.

JUST AS ISRAEL NEEDED TO TAKE ACTION AND SEIZE WHAT GOD HAD ALREADY GIVEN IT, WE TOO MUST TAKE HOLD OF WHAT HAS ALREADY BEEN LEGALLY BESTOWED UPON US IN CHRIST.

I know, I know. *Great . . . another one of those two-sided deals.* But remember the different parts of our makeup—spirit, soul, and body. What is given instantly to one—the spirit—must be possessed over time by the other—the soul. (Again, the actions of the body will be determined by the soul.) Just as Israel needed to take action and seize what God had already given it, we too must take hold of what has already been legally bestowed upon us in Christ. Though our promises and provisions are "Yes" and "Amen" in Him (2 Corinthians 1:20), they will not automatically come to us, just as they didn't for the Jewish people. We also are God's chosen people (1 Peter 2:9) . . . and yet we still need to conquer and subdue the exalted soul with its strongholds.

First Timothy 6:12 speaks of this war, telling us to "fight the good fight of the faith; take hold of the eternal life to which you were called, and you made the good confession in the presence of many witnesses." "Take hold of" is *epilambanomai*, more accurately translated "seize," which gives a sharp image of the intensity and effort involved.[4] Not just reach out and take hold of something—seize it! We must seize the provisions God has given us through His eternal life in our spirit with the vigor of warfare. And with each step God has promised: The inheritance is already ours.

A Great Price for a First Step

Freedom never comes cheap. It always costs something. And yet because it's essential to our well-being, we each face a difficult decision: Are we willing to do whatever it takes, to pay whatever it costs, to gain freedom?

German theologian Dietrich Bonhoeffer knew this cost both in the spiritual realm and here on earth. Imprisoned and tortured during World War II for his Christian faith, this underground church leader was prepared to give his life to denounce the evils that had consumed his country. Just three weeks before his concentration camp was liberated, Bonhoeffer was hanged naked. Yet his cry for freedom and justice was heard in his day and continues to be heard through such powerful statements as this one: "The demand for absolute liberty brings men to the depths of slavery."[5]

In the midst of being persecuted in ways few of us can imagine, Bonhoeffer spoke of a wonderful "slavery." He was referring not to his shackling by the Nazi regime but to our glorious life of service for Jesus. It's the yoke we take for Him. It's the cross we bear daily for His sake. In the last chapter we established that only when we accept "slavery" to Christ can we be truly free. Now we've discovered that the first step toward this freedom—a work in progress—is to believe. Nothing too complicated. No levels of believing or degrees of faith.

It's simply a matter of *Do you believe?* God gifts us with enough faith to believe in His Son for our salvation experience.

Then the question comes: Will our faith grow enough to believe past that? We're out of Egypt; will we take our Promised Land? Do we have the faith to persevere in the fight over our soulish nature? Each of us must answer for ourselves. Like Israel, we must count the cost, knowing what our decision entails. Will we run from our giants and die in the wilderness, or face them and enter into our provision, our inheritance, our rest? The choice is ours.

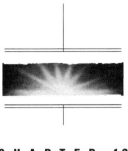

CHAPTER 12

WANTED: TRUE
DISCIPLES

In America, we're touted as a nation of skeptics and cynics. We like to think we won't believe anything until we see cold, hard facts.

I'm not buying it until I see the numbers.

In all seriousness, I don't think we have a problem believing things sight unseen. Recent polls show 92 percent believe in God. Eighty-five percent believe in heaven, while around three-fourths believe hell exists. Another 78 percent believe in angels, and 71 percent say the devil is real.[1]

We don't have a belief problem, we have a practice problem. A live-it-out problem. A walk-the-walk problem. A faith-in-action problem. Polls show this also: Almost 90 percent describe themselves as either "spiritual" or "religious" or both. Yet only half attend worship services weekly (some polls have this fraction as low as one-third). The same number read their faith's sacred text once or twice a month or not at all. While a whopping 85 percent of Americans consider themselves to be Christian,[2] only 16 percent of incoming freshman at Christian colleges are able to explain the basic tenets of their faith.[3] Add to this the embarrassment that a measly 9 percent of born-again Christians tithe on a regular basis.[4]

Clearly we're not following through with what we say we believe. That may be understandable for secular America, but among believers it's a pitiful testament to how poorly we mimic the actions of our Savior. When it all boils down, we have a discipleship problem. And a discipleship problem is a *psuché* problem.

LIVING OUT THE ''D'' WORD

Part of this problem stems from a deficient understanding of discipleship. We've lost touch with the concept Jesus used when He handpicked a dozen men to follow Him in every aspect of life. As one Bible companion explains:

> Whereas a student today studies a subject (law, architecture, or whatever), a disciple in olden days learned from a teacher. Attachment to a specific teacher was the essence of discipleship. The Pharisees and John the Baptist had disciples (Mark 2:18). The Jews saw themselves as disciples of Moses (John 9:28). The term is used often in the Gospels and Acts of the followers of Jesus. They learned from Him and attached themselves wholeheartedly to Him. It meant putting Christ before family and possessions. It meant taking up the cross (Luke 14:26–33). Today, too, to be a disciple of Jesus means total commitment.[5]

Tragically, the church's majority misses out on this call to commitment. Rather than pledge to a lifelong quest of soul renovation that comes from a deep relationship with Jesus, we coast as mere acquaintances of His who happen to be "converted." We are believers, yet we're not disciples. In fact, many of us approach our faith the same way we approached high school, as a necessary requirement, something we endure to get to heaven, rather than investing in it and experiencing fulfillment.

Jesus' ultimate call to action, the Great Commission, doesn't tell us to "Go into all the world and make believers." It doesn't instruct us to get as many converts as possible. Just because we've led a few people in the sinner's prayer doesn't mean we've fulfilled the Great Commission. Jesus commanded us to "go therefore and make *disciples* of all the nations . . . teaching them to observe all that I commanded you" (Matthew 28:19–20). He wants disciples, not converts.

Why is Jesus so passionate about having true followers? The very meaning of the word explains why. The Greek term for disciple is *mathetes*—"a pupil, learner; one who follows both the teaching and the teacher; a follower, imitator; a doer of the teaching."[6]

Catch that last part? I hope so, because it's the key ingredient to being a true disciple: *a doer of the teaching.* Don't think only in terms of obedience, though it certainly has that meaning. As we discussed early on, some Christians are not "doers" because of weaknesses in the soul. In that regard, think of a disciple as one with the desire *and ability* to obey and do Christ's teaching.

James 1:21–25 talks about the man who, after looking in the mirror of God's Word, immediately forgets what he looks like in Christ. In other words, the impression was not lasting. Truth did not sink in. James' point is hit home in verse 22, which tells us to "prove yourselves doers of the word, and not merely hearers who delude themselves." His words are closely tied to Jesus' parable of the sower (Matthew 13:1–23), in which He spoke about the necessity for hearing *and* doing. To be disciples, we must follow both the teaching and the teacher as doers of His Word. Only then are we truly following Him.

ABIDE IN THE WORD: THE HEART OF TRANSFORMATION

Arabian horses go through rigorous training in the Middle Eastern deserts. Trainers require absolute obedience from their horses and test them to see if they are completely trained. The final test is almost beyond the endurance of a living being. A trainer will force the horses to go without water for many days. Then he turns them loose, and they start running toward the water. But just as they get to the edge and are ready to plunge in and drink, the trainer blows his whistle. The completely trained horses that have learned perfect obedience stop, turn around, and come racing back to the trainer. They stand quivering, thirsting, but waiting. When the trainer is sure he has their obedience, he gives them a signal to go back to drink.[7]

This may sound cruel, but when you're in the desert and your life is entrusted to a horse, you'd better have an obedient horse. If we're going to survive the heat of temptation and life's fiery trials, we must accept God's training and obey Him.

> **IN ONE SIMPLE STATEMENT, HE REVEALS THE CRUCIAL STEP BETWEEN BEING A BELIEVER AND A DISCIPLE, TO BECOMING WHO YOU WERE MEANT TO BE—WHO YOU ALREADY ARE IN CHRIST, AND WHO YOU ARE BECOMING IN ACTUALITY.**

In the main passage we'll refer to throughout these last chapters, John 8:30–38, Christ highlights His calling for us to enter into such training and become disciples—dedicated followers and intimate friends. In one simple statement, He reveals the crucial step between being a believer and a disciple, to becoming who you were meant to be— who you *already are* in Christ, and who you are *becoming* in actuality. This may be the most important aspect of everything we've covered so far.

"Then Jesus said to those Jews who believed Him, 'If you abide in

My word, you are My disciples indeed' " (v. 31 NKJV). Let me para-phrase this: "If you abide in My word, you will be able not only to hear My teachings but do them; you will have the ability to follow or imitate Me in every area of your life." That's what we're after!

Abide in My word. Jesus' entire statement hinges upon these words. His promise of complete salvation rests here. In fact, the total resto-ration and transformation of our being centers on the concept of *abid-ing.* This is the crucial step between being a believer and being a dis-ciple. We are to abide in the *logos* (word) of God.

This is the process that produces what Scripture refers to as sanc-tification (1 Thessalonians 5:23), which means to make something holy, or consecrated to God. Abiding is what brings maturity; it grows us up in Him. It is the cocooning process of our metamorphosis, our transformation. Ultimately, this is the road to the freedom Jesus offered, for this is what saves the *psuché* (James 1:21).

Do you get the feeling this is important?

Yes, our initial faith counts toward saving our spirit. And yes, once there, we will live eternally with God in heaven. But the Father's desire is for His life to influence us in the here and now, right where we are. He wants to permeate our entire being and have free reign over every part of us. And that, according to His true Word, is con-ditional to our *abiding in His Word.* If you don't, you will never—never, never, *never*—become who you are!

In Greek, "abide" is *menô*—"to stay in a given place or state, to remain, abide, dwell";[8] "to endure, last; to persevere; to wait for."[9] It is as strong a term as can be found to describe the relationship we need with God's Word. Placing some of the definitions into the phrase gives it added strength:

➤ If you stay in My Word . . .

- ➤ If you remain in My Word . . .
- ➤ If you dwell in My Word . . .
- ➤ If you live in My Word . . .
- ➤ If you persevere in My Word . . .

Can you see the emphasis Jesus is placing on this? He spoke extensively about *menô*-ing in His illustration of the vine and branches (John 15). The branch abides in the vine. It isn't connected to the vine once in a while; it lives there, always attached, ever in that state. If it does not continuously draw its strength and sustenance from the source, it will not bear fruit. James uses *menô* when he speaks of the man who "abides" by the "perfect law, the law of liberty" (1:25). By doing this, he says, we are not forgetful hearers but instead become effectual doers—*disciples*.

We also referred to James talking about those of us who look into a mirror but walk away and forget what the true image looks like. (For some of us, this may be on purpose!) He challenges us not to do this with the mirror of God's Word. One reason we forget what God's Word says we are in Christ, is that we have another mirror, something psychologists call our "looking glass self."[10] We all have an image of ourselves that's based on what's been reflected back to us through events and words. If these come to us frequently enough or are delivered through people or circumstances that impact us significantly, they become what we believe about ourselves. Psychological studies establish that by age five a child has formed a fairly definite self-impression. The same studies reveal that self-esteem is not closely related to social position, family work background, education, or any combination of such factors. A young child sees himself from the reflections of those close to him, mainly his parents.[11]

For example, you may have been told by schoolmates that you

were fat. Perhaps a parent said you weren't wanted or that you were stupid. You may have suffered trauma from abuse or assault. All of what we've heard or experienced combines to create our self-image and become our "looking glass self," our mirror. The beliefs that are formed then control us, whether true or not.

Take Marie, for example. Marie's husband, Jim, thought his wife was beautiful. He told me so before they ever came to me to talk things over. When I saw her, I agreed with him. Jim liked to brag on her to others and never tired of lovingly telling her that she was beautiful. He enjoyed buying her pretty clothes, little love gifts to make her look even more attractive. But in Marie's case, Jim's admiration was causing problems, for her picture of herself was diametrically opposite to what he saw.

"You're only saying that to flatter me," she'd respond. "You don't really mean it."

Jim would feel hurt and frustrated. The more ways he tried to convince Marie that he really thought she was beautiful, the bigger the barrier became.

"I know what I look like," she said. "I can see myself in the mirror. You don't have to make up things like that. Why don't you love me for who I am?" And round and round it went.

Marie's self-concept kept her from thanking God for the gift of beauty. It prevented her from seeing reality. Worst of all, it hindered her from developing a beautiful love-gift relationship with her devoted husband.[12]

Perhaps you've been to a house of mirrors where one makes you look very short and wide, another makes you appear extremely tall and skinny, and others make you seem crooked and wavy. That's what our "looking glass self" does—gives us images of ourselves that aren't accurate. They're distortions: you're a failure, you're unlovable, you can never have self-control. Whether true or not, these perceptions become the mirror by which we live.

Then we're born again. Our spirit becomes brand-new but our soul does not. We start reading and hearing God's Word, which He says is the mirror He wants us to use, and it reflects to us who we now truly are in Christ (2 Corinthians 3:18; James 1:25). But until the mirror already in our soul is transformed, it will trump God's.

> **GOD'S LAW, IF WE ABIDE IN IT, WILL INDEED BRING GENUINE LIBERTY TO OUR SOUL.**

Both James and Paul speak of this in the context of liberty. James calls God's Word the perfect law of liberty. That's another paradoxical phrase sure to enrage and confound the *psuché*. In our thinking, laws don't bring freedom; they restrict and control. Yet God's law, if we abide in it, will indeed bring genuine liberty to our soul.

(Please don't assume at this point that by abiding in God's Word I'm talking about a casual daily Bible reading. And I'm certainly not referring to hearing a weekly sermon. Surely you can see by now— and will understand even more as we continue—that abiding is much more than that. I'm talking about "one who looks intently" [James 1:25]. I'll describe in detail how to look intently, but at this point, understand what this is and isn't in a general sense, and what it will accomplish when done. It's a process so powerful it will allow God to build His very nature into your soul—just the way He intended.)

CHEWING THE WORD

Something as simple as chewing gum can be a relevant analogy to abiding in God's Word. We all have our bubble-gum stories. You know, when your big sister accidentally went to bed with it in her mouth, woke up the next morning with it stuck in her hair, and had to shave her head to get it all out. Or when the third-grade daredevil plied a calcified five-year-old wad from under your chair and, as everyone gagged and gawked, put it in his mouth and acted like it was delicious.

My gum story isn't spectacular or disgusting, but it's certainly stuck with me through the years (pun intended). I could never chew gum for longer than a few minutes. Once the flavor was gone, I couldn't stand chomping on what amounted to plastic cud. My brother, Tim, on the other hand, was a regular cow. He'd start with a piece in the morning and still be working on it by the time he went to bed. During meals, he'd set it on the side of his plate. If he was swimming or doing something else that made it hard to chew, he'd put it back in its original wrapper and save it for later. He always thought I was wasting perfectly fine gum by quickly throwing mine away. (Tim has done numerous things over the years to demonstrate his unique cerebral makeup.)

"Trust me, Dutch, the longer you chew it, the more you get out of it," he'd explain. "Just keep chewing, and it'll be as tasty as when you put it in." Yeah, right.

Of course, because Tim is also older, he had to fulfill his big-brother duties of grossing me out whenever possible. So one day he decided to see if he could chew the same piece of gum for an entire week. Every chance he got, he'd open his mouth in my face, displaying the ever-hardening trophy of his twisted experiment. (Oh, the things we did to amuse ourselves as kids.) I think he eventually made it to Day Three when his jaw gave up.

What in the world does chewing gum have to do with discipleship and abiding? Don't burst my bubble—work with me, okay? When we go to church and listen to our pastor preach on the Word, we're taking in the *rhéma* (spoken words). As we wake up each morning and spend time studying the Bible, we're consuming the *graphé* (written words). But the longer we spend chewing on God's truth, in my brother's terms, the "tastier" it gets. The more we chew, the more *rhéma* and *graphé* become *logos*—the message in the words, the understanding—and this transforms us.

> **GOD'S WORD TEARS DOWN THE EXALTED LIFE-FORCE AND NEGATIVE STRONGHOLDS IN THE SOUL, WHILE AT THE SAME TIME BUILDING INTO IT POSITIVE STRONGHOLDS OF GOD'S LOGIC AND TRUTH.**

When we first hear or read the Word, it's only information competing with other information. At that point we're not getting many nutrients. But as we continue to digest it, the nutrition—the life—begins to feed and change our soul. Jesus said the Word is to us spiritually what natural food is to our body (Matthew 4:4).

As for a cow chewing its cud, that's exactly what we must do with God's Word. Not a pleasant picture, I know, but an ideal illustration. A cow chews, swallows, and brings up the same chunk again and again, working on what's been eaten until all the nourishment is extracted. So it is with God's *rhéma* and *graphé*. We chew them until the Holy Spirit quickens our understanding and nourishes us with the *logos*.

The Amazing Word of God

So how does this process work? When placed in the same quarters as our God-opposing, sinful *psuché*, the *logos* does both a *destructive* and a *constructive* work. God's Word tears down the exalted life-force and negative strongholds in the soul, while at the same time building into it positive strongholds of God's logic and truth. It will both demolish and restore. God's Word is incredibly powerful, as powerful as He is. With it He created everything that exists (Genesis 1; John 1:1–3), holds it all in place (Hebrews 1:3), and one day will destroy all His enemies with the sword of His mouth (Revelation 1:16; 2:16; 19:15). The most literal rendering of Luke 1:37—"Nothing will be impossible with God"—is "No word spoken by God is without power." What a statement! This amazing Word is what He intends to work with to restore our souls.

Let's first address the destructive power of God's Word. Hebrews 4:12 says,

> The word of God is living and active and sharper than any two-edged sword, and piercing as far as the division of soul and spirit, of both joints and marrow, and able to judge the thoughts and intentions of the heart.

God's Word, in its *logos* form—the word used here—can absolutely obliterate anything in its path. It can literally bring something to ruins. And when it comes to transforming us to be more like Jesus and become His true disciples, that's a *wonderful* thing. We're going to take a very thorough look at this verse, chewing until we extract all the awesome flavor.

First, when the writer says God's Word is "living," he uses a form of *zoé*. In other words, this *logos* is alive not just with ordinary life but is energized with God's life. The form used in this verse, *zôa*, means "actively alive." When you digest God's Word, you are receiving His life. Jesus said, "It is the Spirit who gives life; the flesh profits nothing; the words that I have spoken to you are spirit and are life" (John 6:63). God wants to "life" your soul through His Word. Only His life can overcome the spiritual death that took up habitation there. Just as food gives you the necessary nutrients for your body to live physically, ingesting His Word will give you the necessary nutrients to live spiritually.

This verse also describes God's Word as "active," which comes from *energas*. (Notice the word *energy* in it.) Imagine: God's energy working in us! *Energas* also means "to work or toil; operative; effective."[13] So far, with just the definitions of "living" and "active," God says this about His Word: *It is living—actively alive. It is filled with His very life and energy. It toils and works, is operative and effectual.*

How's that for the ability to transform?!

THIS CHANGES EVERYTHING

Joe had an anger problem. Abused as a young boy, he suppressed his emotions at the time. But when he became a teenager, he began to experience bouts of uncontrollable rage. He ran his fists through walls, was known for fighting over seemingly insignificant offenses, and on one occasion intentionally rammed his car into another one. Joe experienced road rage before we had a name for it.

Things went from bad to worse when he married. The first time he grabbed Susan inappropriately. The next time he hit her. That's how they ended up in my office. Susan didn't want to leave him but was understandably afraid to live with him.

Joe didn't want to do what he did in his fits of rage. He just seemed to "lose control," as he put it. By now he had little hope of ever overcoming his anger.

I talked with Joe about his feelings and led him in prayers of forgiveness toward his abuser. We looked at patterns and trigger points until he could recognize the warning signs and pull off by himself. These things helped, but the real breakthrough came as Joe began to attack his problem with the Word.

We found passages on self-control, anger, peace, and other related subjects. Joe began the abiding process, spending time each day thinking on and speaking God's promises concerning his condition. And the living Word began to work on his soul. He began to notice a difference after a few days, which served to encourage him even further. Tenaciously Joe attacked his problems with the Word.

The entire process took a couple of months, but finally the life of God's Word completely swallowed up the stronghold in Joe's *psuché*. He and Susan are still happily married, and he's a big teddy bear. His gentle spirit and kind ways are a tribute to the power and energy of God's awesome Word.

A few other references that speak of God's energy operating in us will encourage you further. Paul says in 1 Thessalonians 2:13 that the Word of God "performs its work [*energeō*] in you who believe." Again, in Philippians, he uses the word three times in two sentences:

> So then, my beloved, just as you have always obeyed, not as in my presence only, but now much more in my absence, work out your salvation with fear and trembling; for it is God who is at work in you, both to will and to work for His good pleasure. (2:12–13)

To better understand, let's put things in the proper order. The first thing to consider is not Paul's charge for us to work out our salvation but that *God is working in us.* God is actively operating in us, releasing His divine life and energy. We already know this has happened in our spirit; now He wants to do the same in our soul . . . "both to will and to work for His good pleasure."

The word *will* is another that's clarified when we discover what word the writer opted *not* to use. There are two words in Scripture that describe when someone "wills" something. The other biblical term for "will," *boulomai* means "deciding something but not pressing on to action."[14] For instance, when you say you'll help a friend move but don't show up on moving day, that's *boulomai*. This happens to us all the time. Ever swore to yourself that you wouldn't eat that second helping of lasagna, or that you'd start exercising, or that you'd stop watching so much TV, or that you'd begin reading the Word more? Oh, the things we wish we'd do . . . but don't. *I promise I'll change. I'm never going to do this again.*

We've all been there. We've all *boulomai*-ed. It doesn't necessarily make us hypocrites—most of us mean these things when we say them. Often we're at our wit's end and are determined to do something to break out of the cycle. But for whatever reason, we don't. We lack what it takes to carry our will through to action.

In contrast to this is the term Paul used, *thelô*, which means "not only willing but pressing on to action."[15] This is when we follow through. Instead of just talking about changing a situation, we go ahead and effect that change. Our actions back up our claim. This is the word used about God working in us to will!

In Word and in Deed

God is working in us (*energeô*) as He releases His power and life not only in our *pneuma* but also in our *psuché*—our will. And He's not merely working in us to muster up enough emotion to try harder next time (*boulomai*); He's literally transforming our will into one that has both desire *and* action (*thelô*). God's energy is active, not passive. He is working in us "both to will [desire] and to work [take action]."

Someone once said the Old Testament brought responsibility but the New Covenant brought response-ability. Israel lived under the yoke of the law; we now live under the yoke of grace. We're not just told to do, we're given the grace to do. As we see here, even when we're oppressed or stuck in our old nature, God is already at work to free us.

Unfortunately, many of us continue to frustrate His grace. We try correcting the situation by relying on our own strength, which keeps us in a cycle of works—trying to save ourselves. But the stone has always been too heavy for us to roll away in our own strength. Still we try, and as a result, we never enter into the rest of Jesus' yoke; we're still living with an Old Testament mindset. Do this, don't do that; be this way, don't be that way. If most of us were honest with ourselves, we'd find we're like the self-flogging monks of the Dark Ages. *You nasty, ugly, despicable Christian, you . . . why can't you be more like Jesus?!*

God says we've got it all wrong.

> *Only my* energeô *can roll the stone away. No other energy can do it.*
>
> *I'm trying to change you from the inside out! I've already made you who you're supposed to be. I stuck My DNA right inside of you, placed My very seed in you. You didn't just get adopted into My family, you were born into My family. You have my nature.*
>
> *Quit trying to fly as a caterpillar. You can't do that. I didn't put wings on him. I made him to transform into a butterfly with glorious wings, just as I've made you with liberation already in mind.*
>
> *If you'll work the process, I will start releasing in you My energy that gives you an entirely new kind of willpower. You won't keep hitting the wall of failure; you'll find yourself committed to action! I'll give you the will to act, and when you act, I'll give you the energy to do it! To will and to do.*

Understanding this, we can now follow through with the charge Paul gives to "work out our salvation with fear and trembling." This doesn't mean we're supposed to "will and do" by our own efforts. God isn't saying, "You're on your own—and do it with fear and trembling because I'm a mean God!" Once again, He already provided the solution to a problem He identified. To "work out" is the word *katergazomai*; the prefix *kat* (from *kata*) means "distribute," and *ergazomai* is another form of the word for "energy" and also means "toiling or working."

Put them together and we can see we are to "distribute the work." Whose work? That's an easy one, since God has already said He's the one toiling in us. And since He's the one at work in us, we are simply to be distributors. He has already placed salvation *in* us, so we can distribute that salvation *out of* us. He is doing it on the *inside* so we can do it on the *outside*. His work is allowing us to become who we are.

And God is doing this by the power of His Word. His Word *is* living and active—"quick, and powerful," as the King James Version states. And it *is* working mightily in you. But there's still much more in this verse. Let's keep chewing.

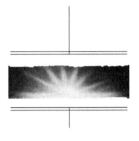

A WORD TO
THE WISE

Words matter. Just ask former chairman of the Federal Reserve Board Alan Greenspan.

At 7:00 on Thursday night, December 5, 1996, at a dinner in Washington sponsored by the American Enterprise Institute, Greenspan gave a speech that to the average person would be nothing more than boring, economic mumbo jumbo. But not to investors with thousands, millions, or billions of dollars in the stock and bond markets.

In what has since become a famous speech, Greenspan uttered ten sentences that in less than an hour began to shake markets around the financial world. The market in Australia, trading at the time, took a sudden nose dive as news of Greenspan's comments came over the newswires; a whopping 2.91 percent of its total value was lost by the end of the trading day. Japan's markets tumbled 3.19 percent, Germany's 4.05 percent. When the New York Stock Exchange opened the next day, the Dow-Jones industrial average almost immediately dipped more than 144 points.

What did Greenspan say? Among other things, he used the word *bubble*, suggesting that the stock market at the time may have been overheated and overvalued by speculation. "One of the nastiest things that can be said about a rising market," wrote Floyd Norris, "is that it's a 'bubble,' conjuring images of a burst that would wipe out most gains in an instant."[1]

Greenspan's comments weren't off-the-cuff ramblings. He was serious about the potential hazards of a booming economy and offered a timely warning for markets worldwide. However, his calculated-yet-loaded words sparked a reaction that, for many investors, left a serious portfolio gouge. Likewise, when we choose to abide in God's *logos*, we set in motion the positive-yet-destructive attribute of His Word. Once again, Hebrews 4:12 describes it thus:

> The word of God is living and active and sharper than any two-edged sword, and piercing as far as the division of soul and spirit, of both joints and marrow, and able to judge the thoughts and intentions of the heart.

The words *living* and *active* have already shown us the incredible way God wants to release its life and energy into us as we abide in His Word. The *logos* doesn't skim the surface; it delves into the core of who we are and, like a medical scanner, reveals the truth of our entire being.

> To better understand the human body, in 1994, researchers made available a new computer tool called "the Visible Man," which consists of almost two thousand computer images. To produce the images, scientists at the University of Colorado Health Sciences Center used a man's body that had been willed to science and took CAT

scans, X rays, and MRI images of it. Then they embedded the body in gelatin. They froze it, sliced it crosswise into 1,800 millimeter-thin sections, and digitally photographed each cross section.

Medical students can look at the Visible Man from any angle, call up an image of any cross section they desire, rotate the images, and put them back together again.[2]

The Word Pierces

In the same way the Visible Man exhibits the body with incomprehensible detail, the Word of God scrutinizes our soul. His word slices and dices, analyzing our motives, priorities, and thoughts. It divides the *psuché* with more precision than any Visible Man can the body, reaching into its deepest parts. The word for this is "piercing"—*diikneomai*, "to reach through, penetrate." It's a compound term; *dia* means "the channel of an act"; *hikanos* means both "to arrive" and "competent, ample, attain the desired end, sufficient, adequate, enough."[3]

Let's put the definitions together and reinsert them into the verse. In fact, let's restate Hebrews 4:12, using all the definitions we've learned so far:

> The *logos* of God is alive—actively alive. It is filled with the life and energy of God. It toils and works in us, is operative and effectual. It is also fully competent, adequate, sufficient, and ample. It has enough ability to channel itself through the various areas of the soul and spirit, reaching its goal and attaining its desired end. It will arrive and will accomplish its goal when it gets there.

Powerful!

Notice especially that it will accomplish its goal once it reaches its destination. Of course, Scripture echoes this truth throughout its pages. In Isaiah 55:11, the prophet relays God's message:

> So shall My word be which goes forth from My mouth; it shall not return to Me empty, without accomplishing what I desire, and without succeeding in the matter for which I sent it.

And God has sent His word to our soul.

Remember the story of Henry Ford and Charlie Steinmetz?

> Steinmetz was a dwarf, ugly and deformed, but he had one of the greatest minds in the field of electricity that the world has ever known. Steinmetz built the great generators for Ford in his first plant in Dearborn, Michigan. One day those generators broke down and the plant came to a halt. They brought in ordinary mechanics and helpers who couldn't get the generators going again. They were losing money. Then Ford called Steinmetz. The genius came, seemed to just putter around for a few hours, and then flipped the switch that put the great Ford plant back into operation.
>
> A few days later Henry Ford received a bill from Steinmetz for $10,000. Although Ford was a very rich man, he returned the bill with a note, "Charlie, isn't this bill just a little high for a few hours of tinkering around on those motors?"
>
> Steinmetz returned the bill to Ford. This time it read: "For tinkering around on the motors: $10. For knowing where to tinker: $9,990. Total: $10,000." Henry Ford paid the bill.[4]

God's Word knows where to tinker. It will penetrate to the needed areas of our *psuché* and release its mighty transforming power once it gets there. Strongholds and their resulting gravestones are no match for it!

The Word Divides

As we abide in God's Word, and as it delves deep into our soul, Hebrews 4:12 says it brings a *division* between what is soul and what is spirit. The word is *merismos*, which means "to divide" and "to apportion."[5] As believers, sometimes we're motivated by our spirit, other times by our soul. Sometimes we're *pneumatikoses*, other times *psuchikoses*. God's Word comes to *divide* the two, making it clear what's spirit and what's soul.

God's Word is a scalpel that skillfully exposes and cuts away unbiblical thoughts and attitudes. It draws a line in the sand, and with great precision says, "This thought or action is *psuché*, that is *pneuma*." Once God has been allowed to shine His spotlight on *psuché*, you'll much more easily recognize *psuché*'s influence in others as well.

Notice that *merismos* also means "to apportion." The Word not only separates soul and spirit but apportions to each part of us the spiritual nutrients we need in order to mature, overcome, and walk in victory. We'll look at an example of this momentarily.

The Word Judges

When the *logos* penetrates to divide and apportion, it has the ability to judge or discern what is good and evil, right and wrong. The Greek word is *kritikos;* you can see the word *critique* in it. Adam decided to judge for himself what was good and evil. He exalted *psuché* and its understanding above God's. By taking in God's Word, we reverse this, allowing Him to be the ultimate Judge. Penetrating the soul, He comes with the searchlight of truth, critiquing all that's there. The psalmist said, "The entrance of thy words giveth light" (119:130 KJV).

In summary, the Word pierces, divides, and judges for a three-pronged purpose:

(1) to expose or identify that which is psuché-initiated versus that which is pneuma-initiated . . .

(2) So that we can (or the word can) properly deal with the psuché (apportion or distribute to it what is needed) . . .

(3) to make us a pneumatikos (spirit-controlled being) rather than a psuchikos (natural- or soul-controlled being).

THIS LIVING LOGOS COMES TO DIVIDE AND CONQUER! AND BE ASSURED, IT WILL GET THE JOB DONE.

In other words, this living *logos* comes to divide and conquer! And be assured, it *will* get the job done.

Earlier I mentioned my struggle with insecurity and fear of rejection. I grew up believing I was ugly, and this shaped my belief system—it became my "looking glass self." Planted deep in my subconscious, this belief gradually came to control all my interactions with others. Up until the eighth grade I was quiet, shy, and, though not disliked, certainly not popular.

Then my family moved to a new school district, and though I'm not really sure how or why, I came out of my shell. Overnight I went from being an introvert to an extrovert. I learned how to relate to others, became popular, and ran with the "in" crowd. Simultaneously

I became a good athlete, and this further augmented my ability to be accepted.

Because of this change, I firmly believed that I no longer suffered from insecurity and fear of rejection. But while I was studying for ministry at Christ for the Nations, God began to deal with me about these issues. I kept hearing Him challenge me to look inward, acknowledge these issues in my soul, and allow Him to heal me.

At first I resisted and adamantly declared my freedom, but the prodding finally became irresistible. At this point I heard Him clearly say to me, *You ARE controlled by insecurity and the fear of rejection, and they influence every relationship you have and color every aspect of your personality. You manipulate and control, put up walls to guard areas of your heart, and all your conversations are subconsciously controlled by your need for acceptance. You don't truly listen in order to know and understand the heart of another person; instead, you're thinking about how you can respond to make yourself look smart, interesting, funny, caring—whatever is needed to make you look good.* (This wasn't an audible voice. Usually when God speaks to me it is through impressions that seem like my own thoughts.)

I didn't like it, didn't agree with it, and told Him so. But God and His Word were relentless—penetrating, dividing, and conquering! His impressions were too strong and persistent—I couldn't get away from them. So I began pondering what I was hearing. Then a strange and unnerving thing began to occur. I would be conversing with a group of people—trying to sound intelligent, funny, "cool," all the things I did in my attempts to be popular and accepted—when I would hear that same inner voice say, *There. You're doing it right now.*

Talk about a bummer of a distraction.

But I began to see that I really was being controlled in my relationships by an inappropriate need for acceptance, not a genuineness that could flow out of a healthy sense of self-worth. I wasn't really interested in what the other person was saying, I just wanted to sound good.

And that wasn't all. I was finally able to see that in all my relationships, I had to be in control. It was devastating. I felt embarrassment, condemnation, and a host of other unpleasant emotions. It seemed I no longer really knew who I was.

I began to talk to the Lord about these feelings, pouring out my shame and confusion. Then I heard Him speak again. *I'm not angry with you, son. It is not your fault that you have these issues. You don't even know how they were formed in you. I do. I'm not disappointed in you, and I don't want you to be embarrassed. I just want to heal you.*

I had never heard God speak to me like that before. My fear of Him began to leave, all the shame lifted, and I just felt loved. He continued: *If you don't allow Me to heal this area of your soul, everything you do in life will be for you—to try to meet your need for acceptance and feel good about yourself. Let me go to work on this.*

I said yes, and God went to work—through His Word.

Somehow I instinctively knew the answer was there. I didn't know *logos* from *psuché*, couldn't have told you one Greek word in Hebrews 4:12, but somehow knew the answer to my freedom was through God's Word. I searched the Scriptures and found verses pertaining to my situation, including references concerning God as my Father; acceptance; His love for me; freedom from fear; and so on.

And while I dove into the Word, another thing began to happen: I started craving it. The more I read, the more I needed it. It may seem like a strange analogy, but when your body needs protein it will do you no good to eat starches or carbohydrates. You must eat foods high in protein. If you're deficient in potassium, you don't seek vitamin C to meet your need; in one form or another, you try to ingest potassium. Somehow your intricately made body knows the difference and sends the nutrients you need to the right place.

So it is with God's Word, the *logos*. It's God's food for our soul. We went on a *logos* fast at the fall, and now we need a *logos* feast. When you need security, you must find portions of His Word that apply and eat them. When you need self-control or discipline, you have to find verses that apply to these things and eat them. When we do this, God's Word will feed our soul the nutrients it needs.

And that is exactly what I did. I took verses pertaining to my situation and began to chew on them. I memorized them, spoke them out loud to myself, and thought about them over and over and over—many times throughout the day. And I did this diligently for days.

The Word began to work. The *graphé* (Scripture) and *rhéma* (spoken word) gradually became *logos* (understanding) as the Holy Spirit lifted the veil from my soul and brought revelation to me. The Word became active in me, releasing power and life. The promises penetrated, found my areas of weakness and injury, and divided and conquered. I didn't heal myself; all I did was eat—abide, dwell in, remain in—God's Word until it saved my soul. His knife went to work, and it hurt so good.

I was free—free indeed. My stone was rolled away and another portion of who God intended me to be emerged from my cocoon. The process probably took a month or so, and I truly was free from the stronghold in my *psuché*. The life in my spirit was finally free to manifest itself through a soul at rest, set free by the truth of God's Word. In that area of my life, I had become who I was.

As the healing came, my entire personality changed. I became quieter, more of a thinker and a listener. My motives changed—I began to relate to people for the right reasons. My desire for success and accomplishment changed. They were now to glorify God, not meet an inappropriate need in me. Performance was replaced with obedience.

Freedom is a good thing!

My *psuché* wasn't so proud or deceived as to believe that God was finished with me at that point. He has and continues to work on areas of my life to bring my soul to the cross. I'm still a *psuchikos* at times, much to my chagrin, but I'm in process. And thankfully, in some areas of my life I am a *pneumatikos*, controlled by my spirit and the Spirit of God.

WARNING: DISTURBING MATERIAL AHEAD (PARTICULARLY FOR YOUR SOUL)

We've been looking at Hebrews 4:12, which describes the destructive aspect of God's Word in relation to our soulish nature and the strongholds residing there. So far, we've seen that the *logos* renders this destruction by penetrating our core, dividing spirit from soul, and judging accordingly. None of this sounds very inviting to the soul, but when we taste the fruit, we realize it really is what we've been looking for, just as happened with me.

In the very next verse, we find even more ominous plans God has for exalted *psuché* and its strongholds:

> There is no creature hidden from His sight, but all things are open and laid bare to the eyes of Him with whom we have to do. (v. 13)

Saying all things are "open and laid bare" isn't exactly a warm and fuzzy thought; that's strong language! The word *open* is *trachelizô*. Part of it, *traché*, is the same root we have in English for *throat*—and for good reason. *Trachelizô*, literally "to seize by the throat or neck,"[6] described bending back the neck and exposing the throat, as with an animal being slaughtered or sacrificed. It was also a battlefield term—need I say more? God has big plans for *psuché*!

In the Old Testament, the high priest would make a sacrifice required by the Lord: He would take an animal and tie its limbs to the four corners of the horns of the altar, then he'd grab the animal by the throat and with one quick slash slit its throat. *Trachelizô*. That blood sacrifice met the obligation and atoned for people's sins, pointing to and foreshadowing Christ's sacrifice.

But here's what most of us have missed: Every time an animal sacrifice was made, it was a picture of God putting the knife to the throat of our *psuché*. Obviously, the sacrifices were pictures of Jesus going to the cross and being sacrificed for us. But why did Jesus endure the cross? To conquer exalted *psuché*. And remember, He said we must identify with Him, daily taking our *psuché* to the cross.

Proverbs 23:2 speaks to this death: "Put a knife to your throat if you are a man of great appetite." Translated literally, it reads, "Put a knife to your throat if you are a man given to soul." Though an analogy of food and appetite, even a cursory look at the context makes it clear the passage is also talking about being controlled by other inappropriate soul desires. If this is happening, put a knife to *psuché*'s throat. Become dead men (and women) walking—living sacrifices.

We'll either accept this knife to the throat or be stiff-necked. If we yield to the knife, we can recognize *psuché* for what it is through revelation by the Spirit and Word, then we can go to the sacrificial altar in agreement that, yes, this soulish nature must be cut open, exposed, and killed. That's what Jesus meant in John 15 when He used the pruning illustration. Just as a gardener prunes the vine branches so they'll produce fruit, our Father cuts us back from time to time—*trachelizô*—so we'll bear His Spirit's fruit (v. 2).

Toward, Not Away

Ask any butcher, sword swallower, or knife juggler: Getting cut never feels good. And having a faulty part of your life hacked off by your Maker's blade probably isn't what you had in mind when you signed up for this discipleship thing. But not every cut is a deep plunge to blatantly remove something. The Father may just need to snip back a weakness or a potential bondage that's holding you back. And when the Lord points out any *psuché* still dominating in you, you're better off flinging yourself on the altar and saving yourself the worse pain of living as a *psuchikos.*

> **OUR BEST BET IS TO TURN TO THE KNIFE RATHER THAN RUN AWAY FROM IT. THAT INITIALLY SOUNDS SADISTIC, YET THE MORE OFTEN WE DO, THE QUICKER WE'LL FIND THAT OUR GOD IS GENTLE, LOVING, KIND, AND MERCIFUL.**

Our best bet is to turn *to* the knife rather than run *away* from it. That initially sounds sadistic, yet the more often we do, the quicker we'll find that our God is gentle, loving, kind, and merciful. He is compassionate and has favor on those who are broken. His cut is ultimately healing, killing only the bad and restoring life to the damaged places.

The Bible mentions several times how it is to our advantage to turn to the pruning ways of our Father:

- ➤ "If you had responded to my rebuke, I would have poured out my heart to you and made my thoughts known to you" (Proverbs 1:23 NIV).
- ➤ "He who falls on this stone will be broken to pieces [this is accepting the discipline]; but on whomever it falls, it will scatter him like dust [this refers to rejecting the discipline]" (Matthew 21:44).
- ➤ "If we judged ourselves rightly, we would not be judged" (1 Corinthians 11:31).

I'd be lying if I said the processes of pruning, brokenness, yield-edness, or discipleship were easy. They're not. They're certainly not comfortable. And they do hurt at times. Yet it doesn't take many instances of God pruning away some of your *psuché* life to know that it's for your benefit and that there's no place you'd rather be than on His operating table. If He can make you in the first place, then He can certainly fashion you into who He created you to be.

> When Australian pastor H. B. Macartney visited Hudson Taylor in China, he was amazed at the missionary's serenity despite his many burdens and busy schedule. Macartney finally mustered up the courage to say, "You are occupied with millions, I with tens. Your letters are pressingly important, mine of comparatively little value. Yet I am worried and distressed, while you are always calm. Tell me, what makes the difference?"
>
> Taylor's response simply pointed to the peace of God that came from continually abiding with His Maker. "He was in God all the time," Macartney later wrote, "and God was in him. It was the true abiding spoken of in John 15."[7]

Hudson Taylor knew all about being pruned and broken. His first eighteen preaching tours throughout mainland China were virtual failures. During his fifty-one years of ministry there, his medical sup-plies (for others) were stolen, taken away, and destroyed; his house was burned down; and his missionary compound attacked, looted, and burned. Eventually, he would bury several children and a wife. Indeed, it seems God allowed this pioneer to be stripped at every turn. Yet Taylor responded not with bitterness but with a yielded spirit, and it led to a greater daily dependence on God. Given the fifty thousand-plus individuals he led to the Lord and baptized, it's obvious he became who God wanted him to be.[8]

Wielding the Knife

Becoming who God created us to be *doesn't* happen overnight. For many believers, the disheartening reality of being cut back and broken to eventually be restored can be almost too much. So it's no coincidence that the writer of Hebrews follows up his ominous statement about the Lord taking His knife to our *psuché* with a powerful word of encouragement:

> Since then we have a great high priest who has passed through the heavens, Jesus the Son of God, let us hold fast our confession. (4:14)

Jesus is the one holding the knife to our *psuché* because He is our great High Priest. He's the only one qualified to make the sacrifice. Remember, He is compassionate and will destroy only what's detrimental to your well-being. As lambs on the altar, we can either struggle against Him or actually help Him wield the knife and allow the process to go much more smoothly.

Yes, we have an important role in the process of sacrificing exalted *psuché*, and this brings us back to the concept of abiding in His Word. About our "hold[ing] fast the confession of our hope," the same phrase is used in Hebrews 10:23, but with different words for "holding fast:" *krateô* and *katechô*. The former puts the emphasis on the strength with which you hold something—holding *fast*. The latter, *katechô*, has several other nuances that spring more from the concept of "holding" something, not so much the force with which it is done. One is "to set or hold to a nautical course; to steer toward."[9] When embarking on a seafaring journey, a navigator would establish the course, and the captain would see that the course was maintained.

It doesn't take much effort to see the spiritual application. We set our course toward God and His liberating truth by abiding in His *logos*, and we stay on course by holding fast to our confession of it. Confession, in fact, is the word *homologia*, which could be defined as "to say the *logos*."[10] "Hold fast to saying the *logos*." When we take God's truth—what He says about us rather than what we think—write it down, study it, memorize it, analyze it, declare it, say it out loud . . . when we apply this kind of diligence and obedience to abiding in and confessing His *logos*, it sets us on a course destined for recovery and freedom.

Speaking God's Word keeps us from wavering (10:23). It prevents us from giving up or jumping ship at the first sight of a storm. There certainly will be storms—we can count on it. The enemy of our soul will come and try to dissuade us. He will use any tactic possible to discourage us, stall us, and get us to veer. At times, we may not even realize we're swerving to the right or left. Yet by abiding continually in and speaking God's *logos*, His Word will keep us safely on course.

Why is speaking or confessing God's Word over ourselves so important? Both Testaments teach that we should do so. (The Old Testament word for "meditate" means not only "to think about" but also "to mutter or speak to one's self.")[11] The only explanation I can give is that God's spoken words are powerful, and He made us in such a way that speaking His Word affects us powerfully:

- Faith comes through them (Romans 10:17).
- Our faith is released through them, causing God's salvation to come to us (Romans 10:10).
- Death and life are released through them (Proverbs 18:20–21).
- They cause us to prosper and have success (Joshua 1:8).
- God's sword, with which we overcome the powers of darkness, is released by them (Ephesians 6:17).

➤ The world and all it contains was made with them
(John 1:1–3).

Many other verses illustrate the power of the spoken word. It's not enough to simply think about it; we must say it.

A BATTLE WITH FEAR

On another occasion while I was a student, I witnessed a horribly gruesome accident. I watched a car lose control on an interstate, go across the median, and hit an eighteen-wheeler head on. The car was slammed end over end for dozens of yards, with the passenger thrown from it but rolling with it. Then, as one of the first to reach the wreckage, I watched as the young man took his final breaths.

This traumatized me horribly, and fear—perhaps a spirit of fear—gripped me. For many days, when I closed my eyes, all I could see was the accident replayed. The fear became so strong that I was afraid to be alone, afraid to walk around the corner of a building, afraid of the dark. For the first time in my life, I understood the verse that says "fear hath torment" (1 John 4:18 KJV). And I couldn't shake it.

My *psuché* was in trouble; a stronghold was forming. I knew I was facing a battle, and if I didn't win, I would struggle with fear all my life. My strategy? First I determined never to yield to it. Whatever I felt afraid to do, I did it anyway. Believe me, that was tough.

Then I went to God's Word and found several verses—it could have been eight or ten, I'm not sure—and began working the process of Hebrews 4:12–14. I meditated on and declared them for days, several times a day. I went to sleep saying them and woke up with them still on the tip of my tongue. I couldn't get to sleep any other way. If I got up during the night, I went back to sleep saying them. I spoke them when I walked, drove, or played. I ate them, chewed them, and wielded them. And they worked in me!

After about two weeks the piercing, dividing, and judging by the Word was complete. It had "lifed" my soul, destroying the stronghold created by the trauma and birthing in me a strength I had never felt. The truth had not only made me free, it had made me strong. I haven't struggled with fear since. If you are struggling to overcome an area of *psuché*, there is no more powerful weapon than God's Word.

Another interesting fact about *katechô*, "holding fast," is that the root from which it's derived, *echô*, is used to describe a pregnant woman. What a great picture for us. What happens if we hold fast to our confession of the *logos* of God? We become pregnant with its truth and can expect to bear fruit!

Remember, our conversion experience involves God implanting us with His very seed, which brings to us His life and nature. Now we're planting the seed of His *logos* into our soul. As we hold fast to it, it grows in us like a baby in an expectant mother. If you ask a woman who's been pregnant what was the greatest thrill of her experience, she'll likely recount the times she felt her baby move inside of her. Likewise, there's nothing more exciting than feeling God's Word begin to work within you.

As we create a safe environment for God's *logos* to develop in us, persevering and holding fast to His implanted Word, we allow it to incubate until it is ready to bring forth life in our soul. Proverbs 4:20–22 summarizes this process:

> My son, give attention to my words;
> Incline your ear to my sayings.
> Do not let them depart from your sight;
> Keep them in the midst of your heart.
> For they are life to those who find them
> And health to all their whole body.

ECHOING GOD

Because so many have heard imbalanced teaching on confessing the Word, let me make a few additional remarks. Unfortunately, the practice of confession has been one of the most misunderstood concepts of the faith. In Hebrews 4:14 and 10:23, the emphasis is not on confessing the sins and weaknesses of our *psuché*, though that's important (see 1 John 1:9). As we stated, it is referring to our confession of the *logos*—God's Word—and what it says about us.

We've already said "confession" is *homologia*, which we defined as "saying the *logos*." Let's break it down further. *Homo* means "same," and *logia* is a form of *logos*, "word." Confession, literally, is "saying the same words." In the context of Scripture it means saying what God says about us. Makes sense, doesn't it? Agree with God! *Homologia* actually has a three-part meaning: (1) assent—agree to the truth of something; (2) consent—submit to it; and (3) expression—pledge to do it.[12]

Let's analyze these one at a time. The first tenet of confession is assent—to acknowledge the truth of something. In our context it would be when the Spirit has finally succeeded in getting us to accept God's knowledge rather than our own. The effects of the fall, exalted *psuché*, are reversed and we accept God's word as truth.

The second tenet is "to consent or submit to something." This is when we not only agree that God's word is truth, we also choose to submit to or obey it.

Finally, confession also means "to state that commitment; to say it." *Homologia* was the word for a promise. When we make a promise, we acknowledge the truth of something, submit to the truth of something, and personally commit to upholding or carrying out that truth.

Putting these three tenets together is what it means to hold fast to our confession of what God's Word says—"I believe it is true, it is true for me, and I declare it to be so."

Permit me to get technical once more. Notice that Hebrews doesn't say to hold fast our *homographé*. In its *graphé* form only (the written word) God's Word doesn't change us. Many people quote verses over and over—I've done so myself—and never see results. Jesus actually said to the Pharisees, "You search the Scriptures [*graphé*] because you think that in them you have eternal life; it is these that bear witness of Me" (John 5:39).

Jesus was explaining that the written Word wasn't producing life for them. Many can quote the Bible; some cult leaders can quote more Bible

WE MUST ALLOW THE HOLY SPIRIT TO MAKE THE WRITTEN WORD THE LIVING WORD.

verses than most Christians. Yet as it was with the Pharisees, in them the Scriptures aren't producing life. Why? The *graphé* must become *logos*. We must allow the Holy Spirit to make the *written* Word the *living* word. As we abide in God's word—and that is the key—the Spirit begins to enable us to truly understand and embrace it. Then we're not just parroting words from a book but feeding on living words from God's heart to ours.

The word for confession is not *homorhéma* either; *rhéma* is simply "spoken words." *Logos* can also mean spoken words, but as you know by now it also includes a comprehension of what they really communicate. Not until we're allowing the Spirit to do His work of giving us understanding, as well as submitting ourselves to it, will our confession—*homologia*—be effective.

This is where so many believers have missed the boat. We've handpicked verses here and there and treated them like lucky charms. "If I take this one and this one and this one, and I speak them aloud enough times, then I'll get my $100,000 . . . or my freedom . . . or my healing."

Such practices simply don't work unless they're grounded in a true relationship with God and His *logos*. We're not meditating on and abiding in His Word when we merely confess a passage over and over again. That's just parroting, and, beyond that, it's often parroting something completely out of context.

I've seen people pass each other "confession sheets" by mail, hoping that by saying a few lines that worked for someone else it will also work for them. It won't, unless the person is working the complete process of abiding. We can never short-circuit the entire abiding process God is trying to take us through.

Confession, in its true intended form, is meditating on God's *logos*, feeding on it, living by its promises, speaking those promises to ourselves and muttering them as we go through our days. It is applying the heart of Deuteronomy 6:6–9 to our every moment:

> These words, which I am commanding you today, shall be on your heart. You shall teach them diligently to your sons and shall talk of them when you sit in your house and when you walk by the way and when you lie down and when you rise up. You shall bind them as a sign on your hand and they shall be as frontals on your forehead. You shall write them on the doorposts of your house and on your gates.

Will the Cutting Ever Stop?!

It should be evident by now that being a true follower of Jesus, a disciple, is all about abiding. And abiding, in turn, is all about allowing the *logos* of God to have its way with our *psuché*. At times, that can be destructive and painful as it delves in deep, cuts away at the soulish nature, and separates the diamonds from the dirt. God doesn't want our soul dominating our being; that's not how He created us to function. We were meant to soar with Him in the spirit realm, with our *psuché* in perfect submission to His breath that flows through us. To get to that point, however, means giving the *logos* permission to destroy the exalted *psuché* nature and existing strongholds that control us.

But the Word also does a constructive work. Rebuilding is what we'll be discussing in the next chapter. And trust me, abiding gets a lot more fun from here on!

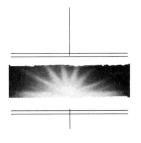

S O W I N G   T H E
S E E D S   O F   G O D

I wanted to be him. Seemed like every guy wanted to be him, but for me it was different. I was determined to model my every move on the football field *and* in life after my hero, Roger Staubach.

He'd done it all. As quarterback for the United States Naval Academy, he'd won the Heisman Trophy his junior year and led his team to the number two national ranking. Following his college career, he stayed true to his military commitment and, rather than asking for a stateside assignment, volunteered for a one-year tour of duty in Vietnam. He ended up waiting five years before playing an NFL game.

Once in the big leagues, however, Staubach thrived. In his first season as starter for the Dallas Cowboys (his third overall), the team won the Super Bowl. He again led them to the title a few years later, as well as to several championship games. But beyond his achievements and accolades, it was the way he played that caught my eye.

Until Staubach came along, QBs often stood in the pocket and picked apart defenses with precision passing. But when "Roger the Dodger" was taking snaps, you knew something more exciting was likely to happen. Staubach was the scrambler of all scramblers. He also had a knack for leading his team to improbable comeback wins. The term "Hail Mary"—now a sports-lingo staple—was introduced after his last-second, fifty-yard bomb stole a 1975 playoff game.

As quarterback for my school team, I set out to play *exactly* like Roger Staubach. I tried to run circles around defenders by scrambling as often as I could. Problem: I wasn't that fast. When I threw, I didn't want to go for easy, rinky-dink three-yarders; I was determined to heave the pigskin as far as I could, every time. Unfortunately, the uncooperative ball regularly ended up either out of bounds or in the hands of opponents (not that my deficient accuracy and lack of arm strength had anything to do with it). And whenever we were behind with only a few minutes left, I became possessed. "Don't worry, guys," I'd tell my teammates. "It's comeback time, baby!"

Needless to say, I was no Roger Staubach. After one season, I gave up my ambitions of playing like him. I'd have to settle for being me.

As a skinny, still-developing teenager, I obviously didn't have the skills, talent, or even the capacity to play like a legend. I needed time—a *lot* of time—and a long list of other attributes even to hope for attaining that level. Walking onto the field with the mindset that I could suddenly become a Hall-of-Famer was misguided.

Yet many of us approach our spiritual growth with similarly foolish expectations. For some reason we think completing a course on inner healing or finishing a study on forgiveness should somehow immediately result in our emergence as masters of those areas. We expect to be overnight legends in the faith when in actuality we're still undeveloped adolescents.

Part of this is positive, in that it's good to desire growth, change, maturity, results. Part of it, though, is that we frequently want results without embracing the process that will yield them. Maybe you've hoped that after reading this book, you'll finally have "arrived" at a place of lasting freedom. Perhaps something deep in you continues to whisper, "This is *it*! This is finally the answer to my soul problem. Now I can shake off my strongholds and bondages and handle my issues. I'll finally be who God wants me to be."

Don't worry, I'm *not* criticizing the desire for permanent results. That's a wonderful thing. And I certainly don't discourage high expectations. But I must remind you, once again: It ain't gonna happen overnight.

In the same way that we long for the "finished product," we also need to undertake and embrace a passion for the *path*, the journey, to our completion. As I said earlier, God's purpose and intent is for you to be who He made you to be—who you are. And we can also know this: Because God is God, His way is best. If it were better for us to instantly "become" than to walk the road of becoming, no doubt that's how He would enable us to experience it. In this vein, faith is believing that what God says is true; obedience is conforming to His means just as much as to His ends.

Let me assure you, if you keep abiding and abiding and abiding, it *will* happen. The truth *will* make you free. Why? Because God's Word has a perfect track record. Once more:

> So shall My word be which goes forth from My mouth;
> it shall not return to Me empty, without accomplishing
> what I desire, and without succeeding in the matter for
> which I sent it. (Isaiah 55:11)

That's His promise, not mine.

In the last chapter we learned about the *destructive* aspect of His *logos;* in this chapter we get to see its *constructive* facet. God does not destroy areas of our *psuché* just for the sake of tearing something down. He has rebuilding plans that far surpass our wildest dreams!

Just as it is written: "Things which eye has not seen and ear has not heard, and which have not entered the heart of man, all that God has prepared for those who love Him." For to us God revealed them through the Spirit; for the Spirit searches all things, even the depths of God. (1 Corinthians 2:9–10)

"I know the plans that I have for you," declares the Lord, "plans for welfare and not for calamity to give you a future and a hope" (Jeremiah 29:11).

Good things await!

Small Beginnings, Big Results

Several years ago the Lord spoke something to me that was one of the greatest revelations I've ever received. I was talking to Him about why the Word wasn't working in me. Truth be told, I was complaining about seeing a lack of fruit in my life. I'd sat under countless great teachers, listened to all the right tapes, read all the classic books, and all I heard was how I was supposed to be victorious. I was supposed to walk in perfect health and have a sound, disciplined mind. I was supposed to overcome, never be depressed, never get discouraged, always be consistent, flourish in joy . . . on and on it went. So I aimed for those results. And my heart had pure motives. I wanted to be used by God to the best of my abilities.

Some nights I thought I was mere inches away from attaining this "I've arrived!" state. I'd leave church services and prayer meetings high on hope. "Yes! Now *that* is what I needed!" I'd say after another amazing revelation. "This will finally bring permanent change. I'll never be the same!"

A few days later and, you guessed it, I was the same.

"God, why isn't this working for me?" I cried out. I was pretty upset, feeling like a complete failure. And then He spoke in one of those ultra-clear voices that only happens a few times in your life. Not audible, but just as powerful. And without doubt it has been one of the most important things I've ever learned.

Because all truth comes to you in seed form.

Huh? (Really, that's what I said.)

He continued: *For those people who are teaching you—the ones who are giving you all these testimonies of what's worked for them—that truth is fruit in them now. But it isn't transferred to you as fruit. It comes to you as a seed. Whether it bears the same fruit in you depends on what you do with it, because all truth comes in seed form. If you do what they did and abide in My word, that seed will grow in you also, and the truth will make you free, just as it has for them.*

I chewed on this for a while. I began to think of all those I knew who were clearly bearing fruit in certain areas of their lives. I thought of a young man who had been horribly scarred by drugs. He'd used so many that his mind was "fried"—damaged. He gave his heart to Christ and immediately began to immerse himself in God's Word. And I do mean immerse—he spent hours every day reading, meditating upon, memorizing, and speaking Scripture. Sure enough, after a few months, not only was this young man *completely* free of any temptation toward drugs, his mind was completely healed. In fact, I'd say he was brilliant.

I recalled another young man who'd come out of a lot of bad "stuff"—he was a really good sinner. Not only did he get free of the sin strongholds in his life through abiding in God's Word, but he experienced a freedom of a completely different kind: He was set free from a poverty mentality. Coming from an extremely poor background, he firmly believed he would always be poor. And he was proving it. He couldn't keep a job, was always lacking money, never had anything nice—you get the picture.

Then he heard a man speak on true prosperity, being blessed by God to be a blessing. So he found several Scriptures on God's provision, sowing and reaping, etc., and began to feed and meditate on them. He did this for days, then weeks and months. You guessed it. Before long that stronghold was broken and in its place was an incredible faith for finances. He became one of the most prosperous men I know … and one of the biggest givers.

YOU HAVE TO WORK THE PROCESS. INFORMATION SEEDS MUST BECOME FRUIT-PRODUCING REVELATION.

As I pondered these examples in the context of what God had said to me, I could immediately see the truth of what I'd heard from Him. It became what I call "the seed principle." The concept of a seed indicates *a process of growth until fruition.* Suddenly I knew I couldn't expect freedom while short-circuiting the process. In the same way, you can't presume to gain freedom in problem areas of your life if you haven't abided in God's *logos* regarding those areas. Let me be blunt: Reading this book doesn't mean you'll be any freer in certain areas of your life. You may understand a lot more about how to *get* free, but you won't automatically *be* free when you finish the last page. You have to work the process. *Information* seeds must become fruit-producing *revelation.* And for that to happen, you have to tend the seed.

He Who Comes to Steal, Kill, and Destroy

This is nothing new. As much as I'd love to take credit for the idea of nurturing a seed with the *logos* until it becomes fruit, the concept is straight from the Bible's pages. Matthew 13, Mark 4, and Luke 8 all recount the parable of the sower in which Jesus talks in detail about this seed principle. He indicates that the maturity of the seed—His word in us—is a growing process. And if that seed is nurtured, just like a natural seed, it will grow to fruition. Yet He also mentions a valuable truth of which we all need to be acutely aware as we tend to our seed: Satan will try to steal or destroy that seed at all points along its progression.

Mark 4:15 proves that Satan often attacks *immediately:*

> These are the ones who are beside the road where the seed is sown; and when they hear, immediately Satan comes and takes away the word which has been sown in them.

At other times, the devil attempts to thwart our growth *before the root system is well-developed:*

> In a similar way these are the ones on whom seed was sown on the rocky places, who, when they hear the word, immediately receive it with joy; and they have no firm root in themselves, but are only temporary; then, when affliction or persecution arises because of the word, immediately they fall away. (vv. 16–17)

Catch that secondary point? Trouble or persecution will come—we all know it. But Jesus directly links this trouble to the Word of God: "Affliction or persecution arises because of the Word." God's *logos* incites the wrath of fallen Lucifer and of our fallen nature. Our logic hates when it's forced to bow the knee to God's logic. And when that occurs, Satan is all too willing to come alongside in agreement and stir up trouble. By the very nature of this conflict, we can expect the process to be tested—just like it was for Slick.

His real name was Steve, but he liked to call himself Slick, so I'll stick with that. Slick had one of the most dramatic conversions I've ever witnessed. He literally ran to the altar to give his heart to Christ. Tears, hugs, high fives, and hallelujahs were the order of the night as Slick's friends and family celebrated with him his entrance into true life.

Things went well for several weeks. Slick seemed completely transformed. He wasn't. The life in his spirit had not yet fully arrived in his *psuché*. Slick didn't understand this, he just figured he was "saved."

Then this newborn convert met someone else with the same name. Slick number two is first mentioned in Genesis 3:1:

> Now the serpent was more crafty than any beast of the
> field which the Lord God had made. And he said to the
> woman, "Indeed, has God said, 'You shall not eat from
> any tree of the garden'?"

"Crafty" is the Hebrew term *aruwm,* from the root *aram,* which means "to be bare, to be smooth."[1] That's right—slick. The concept of a person being a "smooth operator," slick in their ability to deceive or connive, is found in this word. Satan's cunning and craftiness are his greatest weapons. It is, in fact, the first thing Scripture says about him.

Slick was no match for Slick.

Satan knew something this young believer didn't: He still had an ally in the man's *psuché* that wasn't being dealt with by God's *logos.* The truth in Slick's soul was still in seed form. It wasn't even that hard, really. Satan just waited for the excitement to wear off of Slick's emotions, and one day, at just the right time, when his defenses were down, "arranged" a meeting with Slick and his former dealer. Before long, his addiction was back in full swing, disillusionment set in, and another new "convert" to Christ was lost.

I was just as confused as everyone else. Slick seemed so genuine and his salvation experience so real. Not until years later when God led me into this study did I begin to understand what had happened. Make sure you tend your seed!

The enemy of our soul will also do whatever it takes to stunt the maturation of our seed *at any point.* Mark 4:18–19 explains:

> Others are the ones on whom seed was sown among the thorns; these are the ones who have heard the word, but the worries of the world, and the deceitfulness of riches, and the desires for other things enter in and choke the word, and it becomes unfruitful.

Whether through fear, financial stress, lust ... whatever the issue, Satan will try to bait us all along the way. His primary goal is to get us to abort the process so he can steal the seed. And we can be sure that his attacks will be well-timed—sneaky, conniving scoundrel that he is!

After more than forty-five years of marriage, Focus on the Family's James Dobson has earned the right to be one of the nation's leading voices for defending the institutions of both marriage and family. Yet he's also endured his share of attacks from Satan on the very thing he stands for. In *Life on the Edge*, he recounts a particularly well-timed ploy.

> Shirley and I had been married just a few years when we had a minor fuss. It was no big deal, but we were both pretty agitated at the time. I got in the car and drove around for about an hour to cool off. Then when I was

on the way home, a very attractive girl drove up beside me in her car and smiled. She was obviously flirting with me. Then she slowed down, looked back, and turned onto a side street. I knew she was inviting me to follow her.

I didn't take the bait. I just went on home and made up with Shirley. But I thought later about how vicious Satan had been to take advantage of the momentary conflict between us. The Scripture refers to the devil as "a roaring lion … seeking whom he may devour" (1 Peter 5:8 KJV). I can see how true that description really is. He knew his best opportunity to damage our marriage was during the hour or two when we were irritated with each other. That is typical of his strategy. He'll lay a trap for you, too, and it'll probably come at a time of vulnerability.[2]

Problems From Within

Besides Satan's scheming, there are other pitfalls that can cause us to abort the seed-like process of abiding in God's *logos*. With equally disastrous results, each of these stems not from an outside source but from our own *psuché*. In other words, not only do we need to watch out for our enemy's deterrent ways, we also should beware of our own. There are certainly others, here are three pitfalls that most seed-tenders encounter.

(1) Trying to Transform Ourselves
Obviously we have a part in the transformation of our soul. If we want freedom, it's up to us to act on the five steps we're in the process of outlining: believing, abiding, knowing the truth, being free, and being free indeed. However, the bottom line is that we're not responsible for our redemption; Jesus already took care of that on the cross. If we could execute such a transformation, if *psuché* could save *psuché*, this book wouldn't need

to be written! But left to our own devices and methods of saving ourselves, we fail 100 percent of the time.

Thankfully, God provided the way to our complete, assured transformation. Knowing and believing in the sacrifice Jesus already made to ensure our liberty, our main task now is simply to abide in His *logos*. We don't strive to be, but to become who we already are—from the inside out.

> **WE'RE NOT RESPONSIBLE FOR OUR REDEMPTION; JESUS ALREADY TOOK CARE OF THAT ON THE CROSS. OUR MAIN TASK NOW IS SIMPLY TO ABIDE IN HIS LOGOS.**

(2) Focusing on the Problem   Unfortunately, rather than spending our energy on abiding, we get sidetracked by the dilemma we're facing. A molehill easily becomes a mountain when stared at for too long. So it is with our soul's crisis. Staring at the stone, obsessing over the stone, yelling at or pleading with the stone . . . no amount of focus on the stone moves it. The stone is the problem; we need the solution.

For example, a friend of mine from Ohio had been a smoker for more than thirty years. He was a great Christian brother who repeatedly and honestly wanted to quit but never could. One day he called me for help. I could tell he was at the end of his rope, completely frustrated with his inability to "fix" the problem. Yet he'd been at this place so many times he didn't know what to do anymore.

"Get your mind off of it," I told him. "Seriously, quit fighting and just relax. I know that sounds crazy, but you've got to realize that you're already accepted by God. He's not against you in this fight,

He's for you. So just ease up and don't focus on your problem, focus on your Problem-Solver."

I began to describe to my friend the "law principle" that I saw at work in his life. The law came to show us our inability (Galatians 3:23–25; Romans 7:7–9), not make us righteous. By its very nature, it makes us inept failures because it presents a standard we can never live up to. Romans 5:20 says, "The Law came in so that the transgression would increase." In other words, God knew we couldn't obey it. But He wanted us to know it. So He set us up to fall on our face: "I was once alive apart from the Law; but when the commandment came, sin became alive and I died" (7:9). The more we focus on the commandment, the more we're going to see our weakness and fail. When we function out of the law, our sin nature is awakened, which only causes our falling and stumbling to increase.

My friend was definitely caught in a mesmerizing trance of staring at his problem. He had become tunnel-visioned because the obstacle seemed too overwhelming. All he could see was his inability. And so I continued my advice, this time getting even more radical.

"Your main objective right now is simply to rest in God's Word. Abide in it." (He had listened to my teaching on abiding and knew exactly what I was talking about.) "Go to the Bible and start meditating on the Scriptures God has given you that say you're more than a conqueror, that you *can* do this, that the One who is in you has already overcome this world. Find verses that talk about discipline, self-control, being more than a conqueror. Plant the seeds. Think on them, say them, and rest in His comforting words. And as you start this abiding process, just relax. Don't worry about the problem—even while you're smoking a cigarette, don't worry about it! Talk to God while you're doing it, and thank Him for delivering you through His Word. I'm completely serious. Don't be condemned. As you rest in the faithfulness of God's Word coming through with its promises, you'll find that that's exactly what happens. I assure you."

My words connected deeply with my friend. He had fallen in a trap of trying to change himself from the outside in. And in his earnest desire to quit smoking, his struggle became bigger and bigger as he tried in his own strength. Eventually, he couldn't keep his eyes off the problem.

Three months later, he called me up and told me the news. He'd done exactly what I said, and one morning he simply woke up and decided he didn't like smoking anymore. The guy hasn't had a cigarette since. Pretty miraculous, yet simple. All he did was follow the instructions of God's Word. His story truly shows the second half of that verse in Romans:

> The law was added so that the trespass might increase. *But where sin increased, grace increased all the more,* so that, just as sin reigned in death, so also grace might reign through righteousness to bring eternal life through Jesus Christ our Lord. (5:20–21 NIV)

(3) Denying the Problem   Denial is never a good option. Yet sadly that's where so many Christians have decided to live.

> On February 9, 1996, a railroad train in New Jersey ran through a red signal and smashed into the side of another train at a crossing. The crash killed the engineers of both trains and one passenger, and injured 158 other passengers.
>
> One year later the National Transportation Safety Board announced the results of its investigation into the cause of the accident. The engineer of the train that ran the red signal was going blind. According to the *New*

York Times, for nine years the engineer had progressively been going blind because of diabetes. He and his doctor both knew it. But he had kept his medical condition secret, no doubt for fear of losing his work, and the doctor, who reportedly knew that his patient was a railroad engineer, had not reported the man's condition to the railroad.

New Jersey requires that its engineers have a physical exam each year by the company's own occupational medicine specialist, but each year the engineer had "always answered no to the annual questions about whether he had diabetes, was taking any prescription medication, or was under another doctor's care. He'd had eye surgery twice but apparently paid for it out of pocket rather than filing insurance claims.

Unfortunately, the truth came out in a deadly way.[3]

Rather than denying the obvious and pretending we can keep the truth hidden even from ourselves, we can embark on a simple three-step process I like to call ACT:

> A—Acknowledge the facts. Don't run from or try to deny the existence of your problem. And acknowledge your inability to overcome it in your own strength. It's a basic truth: Identifying the problem puts it out in the open, exposing it. You must bring it out from the darkness, which is Satan's domain. The more we keep things in the light, the less sway our enemy has.

> C—Choose to exalt God's Word and truth, not *psuché.* Seems simple enough ... and it is. But remember, truth comes as a seed. And freedom isn't a simple choice. What is chosen is the *process* of freedom: believing and abiding in the truth of God's Word

rather than what *psuché* tells us. A great example of this is the story of Abraham fathering a son at an old age:

> Without becoming weak in faith [Abraham] contemplated his own body, now as good as dead since he was about a hundred years old, and the deadness of Sarah's womb; yet, with respect to the promise of God, he did not waver in unbelief but grew strong in faith, giving glory to God, and being fully assured that what God had promised, He was able also to perform. Therefore also it was credited to him as righteousness. (Romans 4:19–22)

Abraham didn't deny his condition. He acknowledged his old age and his soul's inability to believe God's promise any longer. After all, he'd waited almost twenty-five years. But he also chose to exalt God's word and work the process that overcomes the weaknesses of the soul. Why do I assert that he had unbelief to overcome when in Romans Paul says he didn't waver or grow weak in his faith? Abraham actually did come to an unwavering level of faith by the time Isaac was conceived. But up until God's final announcement that they would have a son, both he and Sarah *were* wavering.

How do we know this? According to the Old Testament account, one year before Isaac was born Abraham and Sarah were in utter disbelief that they could conceive. Both of them laughed cynically at God for saying it would still happen, and Abraham practically begged God to allow Ishmael, his son through Hagar, to fulfill the promise (Genesis 17:15–21; 18:10–15).

Does Scripture contradict itself? Do Romans and Genesis disagree? Not at all. Abraham "grew strong in faith" until he was "fully assured" (Romans 4:20–21). He didn't start with strong faith. And here is a very encouraging point: If both Abraham and Sarah were in blatant unbelief exactly one year before Isaac's birth but were in strong faith when he was conceived (as this passage and Hebrews 11:11 emphatically states), then in three short months they went from weak faith to strong faith. That should reassure you! Abraham, our spiritual father, had faith issues at one point just like most of us. Don't be condemned if you're struggling with a promise. If in three months he and Sarah went from no faith to great faith, so can you!

Growing strong faith need no longer be a mystery. Faith comes through the seed principle. *Graphé* (the written word) and *rhéma* (the spoken word) are tended until they become *logos* (the living, understood word). Revelation. Seeds have been planted, watered, guarded from insects and weeds, and given the proper nutrients until they turned into fruit. Again, information seeds become fruit-producing revelation. In this case, that's faith.

> T—Take action. Sure, there's a fine line in the abiding process between allowing the Lord to do His work in us and being diligent with our own efforts. The key, however, is to strive or work at the process of abiding, not at changing ourselves.

Progress, Progress, Everywhere

If you can't already tell by my penchant for translations and word definitions, I'm a teacher at heart. And so I realize that abiding, this second step in the freedom process, can seem overwhelming simply because of the breadth of content we've covered. To make things clear, let's quickly review. (And no, there won't be a quiz at the end. Tell *psuché* not to cram.)

In the last two chapters, we talked about how Jesus said being a true disciple means abiding in His Word. We saw that His *logos* is a powerful force that destroys exalted *psuché* and its strongholds. And in this chapter we've touched on the various ways that restoration—

the constructive aspect of abiding—takes place. As with a seed planted in hopes of producing fruit, it's essential that we tend to the seed of God's *logos* within us so that it fully matures. In fact, if we don't take such care, there are numerous forces, including our own *psuché*, ready to abort the maturation process.

Jesus mentioned these various tragic scenarios in His parable of the sower. As we read earlier, God's Word can end up stolen by scavengers (Matthew 13:4). It can be thrown among the rocks and start strong but quickly fizzle out for lack of proper nourishment (v. 5). And it can end up in a hostile environment that isn't receptive to it in the first place (v. 7). But when the *logos* lands in the right place and is properly tended to, it flourishes. In fact, it does exactly what it's supposed to do and bears an abundance of fruit.

For even further review, let's see how Jesus summarized getting to this ideal state:

> The one on whom seed was sown on the good soil, this is the man who hears the word and understands it; who indeed bears fruit and brings forth, some a hundredfold, some sixty, and some thirty. (Matthew 13:23)

First, according to this verse, the natural progression of abiding begins with "hearing" the word. In other words, we receive either the spoken word (*rhéma*) or the written word (*graphé*). God speaks through both means, so it's not important exactly how we receive His word. At this point, it's only seed.

Second, once we hear His word, Jesus said we then must understand it. *Suneimi* means "to put together."[4] We often say when understanding of something has finally occurred, "the pieces came together." That's what God does for our soul—in a sense He integrates it with Him. He mixes His knowledge into ours and we "understand" truth. This process is enhanced by the tools of abiding—meditating on the Word, memorizing it, singing it, writing it out, declaring it, and so on. These are all ways we can protect and care for the seed. As we do, the Spirit eventually brings true understanding—revelation. The word has become *logos* to us.

Third, Mark's account reveals another step in this abiding process: acceptance. "Those are the ones on whom seed was sown on the good soil; and they hear the word and accept it and bear fruit, thirty, sixty, and a hundredfold" (4:20). This word *accept* means "to receive and embrace with assent and obedience." We must embrace the *logos*, cherishing it as we would a loved one. Jeremiah said, "Your words were found and I ate them, and Your words became for me a joy and the delight of my heart" (Jeremiah 15:16). Author, teacher, and pastor Harry Ironside embodies this:

> Under his mother's guidance, Ironside began to memorize Scripture when he was three. By age fourteen, he had read the Bible fourteen times, "once for each year." During the rest of his life he continued to read the Bible through at least once a year. A pastor recalled a Bible conference at which he and Ironside were two of the speakers. During the conference the speakers discussed their approaches to personal devotions. Each man shared what he had read from the Word that morning. When it was Ironside's turn, he hesitated, then said, "I read the book of Isaiah." He was saturated with the Word of God.[5]

"Assent to it" and "obey it" are also part of the meaning of "accept" in this verse. This, remember, is a part of biblical confession—assenting and saying. We must embrace, cherish, declare, and obey the Word.

Fourth, we can also count on facing attempts to thwart this growth process. Storms will come to disrupt and challenge our maturation. Luke thus adds the warning that we must *hold fast* in our tending to the seed: "The seed in the good soil, these are the ones who have heard the word in an honest and good heart, and hold it fast, and bear fruit with perseverance" (8:15). This is consistent with what we found in Hebrews: "hold fast our confession"; "hold fast the confession of our hope" (4:14; 10:23).

In summary, when we persist in nurturing the *logos*, revelation will come to enlighten and bring truth to us (Ephesians 1:17–18). If attended to (Proverbs 4:20), guarded (4:23), continued in (John 15; James 1:25), and meditated upon (Joshua 1:8; Psalm 1:1–3), the word of God will bear the fruit He has promised. Galatians 6:9 offers the perfect encouragement:

> **WHEN WE PERSIST IN NURTURING THE LOGOS, REVELATION WILL COME TO ENLIGHTEN AND BRING TRUTH TO US.**

> Let us not lose heart in doing good, for in due time we
> will reap if we do not grow weary.

Our goal is to see our *psuché* transformed to the point that we are bearing healthy fruit. We want a harvest in the soul. Usually we hear the phrase "harvest of souls" and associate it with evangelism. While that's certainly wonderful, let's not forget that God is not after a wave of converts. He's after disciples—redeemed souls that now have His living, breathing, spirit-filled *logos* at work in them. *Pneumatikoses.* And the more we abide in His Word, the closer we get to that discipleship becoming a way of life.

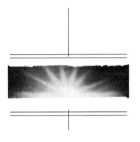

CHAPTER 15

KNOWING YOUR
WAY TO FREEDOM

In the John 8 passage upon which we're basing our five-step process of freedom, Jesus states, "If you abide in My word, you are My disciples indeed. And you shall know the truth, and the truth shall make you free" (vv. 31–32 NKJV). We've already covered the first two steps—believe and abide; now let's examine what it truly means to *know the truth and be free.* Actually, most of the work is done. What we'll discuss in this chapter—the last three steps—are the results of continuing the abiding process.

For some students in the Dallas-Fort Worth area, knowing the truth wasn't so easy. A review by the Texas Education Agency of state-standardized test scores in 2005 revealed a potential statewide cheating scandal that in particular highlighted notoriously low-scoring elementary schools on Dallas's southeast side. Overall, one in twelve public schools—elementary, middle, and high schools—showed unusual results that suggested some form of cheating during the year. Those signs ranged from an extraordinary spike in scores to an uncanny similarity among test answers to identical answer sheets. However, one of the most disturbing trends discovered through previous years of investigation was the number of alleged teachers found changing students' answers after tests had been administered.[1]

Now, I'm no genius. But I do know that when you've got *teachers* cheating on tests for students' sake, there's a serious problem. Talk about out-of-control *psuché*! What struck me about this story wasn't the degree to which some people will go to ensure a better scholastic future or potential scholarship possibilities. No, it's that those kids involved (whether they or their teachers did the actual cheating) have no idea what the real answers should've been. They couldn't tell you the truth from their number-two-pencil-erased miscalculations. Their knowledge is faulty and full of errors, yet they're moving on to a higher level of learning simply because they scored a passing grade. Meanwhile, what they know is flat wrong.

We suffer from a similar dilemma as *psuché*-dominated humans. In our mind, we've got all the right answers to our soul's problems. And there's no chance *we* could be wrong, now, is there? Ever heard someone labeled "too smart for his own good"? That's appropriate for all of us who can't dumb it up enough to recognize our own deficiency and inability.

Got Smarts, or Got Truth?

Fortunately, Christ waded through our pride and pseudo-intelligence and proclaimed His solution—the real answer—to our problem. *If you will abide in My logos, you will know the truth.* What was lost at the fall will be restored. The third stage in our progression toward freedom is knowing the truth. The word *know* comes from *ginôskô*, a threefold knowledge that by definition is relational, progressive, and effectual.[2] It involves intimacy, is an ongoing process, and has an effect on the one doing the knowing. When these definitions of knowing are plugged into Christ's words, they take on new meaning. They embody the process we've been explaining.

That's a far cry from exalted *psuché*'s version of knowing. Remember *Rain Man*? It was based on the life of possibly one of the world's most outstanding minds, Kim Peek. The fifty-six-year-old could read a separate page of text with each of his eyes. He could scan a page in ten seconds and retain every bit of information. He memorized entire phone books in a matter of hours, was a certified expert in fifteen different

THE WORD *KNOW* COMES FROM *GINÔSKÔ*, A THREEFOLD KNOWLEDGE THAT BY DEFINITION IS RELATIONAL, PROGRESSIVE, AND EFFECTUAL. IT INVOLVES INTIMACY, IS AN ONGOING PROCESS, AND HAS AN EFFECT ON THE ONE DOING THE KNOWING.

fields, and could recall facts from almost ten thousand different books.³ And yet, without slamming Peek simply for having a God-given gift of über-intelligence—I'm thoroughly impressed—you have to wonder: What difference do all those smarts make on his soul? If any of us decided to embark on a lifelong journey to become the world's most intelligent person, would it get us any closer to heaven? Would it cause us to connect more with the spirit realm, where things *really* matter? Nope. Intellectual knowledge won't save us, contrary to what *psuché* and its "institutions of higher learning" assert. God says, "Knowledge makes arrogant [literally "puffs up"], but love edifies" (1 Corinthians 8:1).

I'm not in any way condemning education. And I'm certainly not implying that there's no point in trying to use our brains to their fullest capacity. I'm just not impressed with exalted *psuché*—humankind's knowledge apart from God. Man's idea of knowledge, which is essentially a matter of how smart you are, has little to do with what Jesus was speaking about in John 8:32. God is concerned about truth. Eternal, everlasting truth that outlives the latest technological discovery or political trend.

The Bible describes this kind of knowledge as *epignôsis*, as in 2 Peter 1:3:

> His divine power has granted to us everything pertaining to life and godliness, through the true knowledge of Him who called us by His own glory and excellence.

The New Testament writers frequently used this term to describe knowledge of things both ethical and divine. Within it we can see the root, *gnôsis*, that's also found in *ginôskô*. In other words, it's a precise knowledge that combines the best of man's intelligence and God's wisdom. It abides and is enveloped in the truth—*alétheia*—that Jesus refers to.[4]

As expected, our *psuché* isn't naturally a fan of this *epignôsis* knowledge. It would rather be bloated intellectually. It would rather identify a problem and have it solved within a single counseling session. None of this long, drawn-out, abiding stuff. This is true even for believers. We prefer to have instant healing—or, if it's not instant, we'd at least like it out of the way within a neatly packaged eight-week course.

I'll say it again: God doesn't work that way. Jesus' emphasis is one of abiding and *ginôskô*-ing. We must continually—daily, hourly, minute-by-minute—reside in the truth of God's *logos*. Only then do we enter into the results that everyone's been waiting for . . .

FREEDOM!!!

Picture a lean, gangly, bearded man standing at a podium. He's addressing a crowd small in numbers but nonetheless invaluable in his eyes. These are the fathers and mothers of soldiers who just weeks earlier had lost their lives on this very spot. And as only a president can do, Abraham Lincoln is honoring the memory of those brave young men by reminding everyone present of the inspiration that fueled the fires of their courage. He speaks of loyalty, valor, and strength. Most of all, he speaks of their ultimate cause: freedom.

> Our reliance is in the love of liberty which God has planted in us. Our defense is in the spirit which prized liberty as the heritage of all men, in all lands everywhere. Destroy this spirit and you have planted the seeds of despotism at your own doors. Familiarize yourselves with the chains of bondage and you prepare your limbs to wear them.[5]

After meeting with each parent individually and expressing his sincere condolences and appreciation, Lincoln addresses the entire group once more, offering both a charge to the future and a reminder of the past:

> Freedom is the natural condition of the human race, in which the Almighty intended men to live. Those who fight the purpose of the Almighty will not succeed. They always have been, they always will be, beaten.[6]

(Including Satan and *psuché*, I might add.)

Now picture a hillside in the Scottish highlands, where a thousand-deep lineup of scraggly men dressed with rugged kilts and painted faces stand on the brink of battle against a pristine English army. The Scots' notorious commander, William Wallace, is mustering his makeshift troop of volunteer fighters and reasoning with those tempted to abandon the conflict.

Aye, fight and you may die, run, and you'll live . . . at least
for a while. And dying in your beds, many years from
now, would you be willin' to trade *all* the days, from this
day to that, for one chance—just one chance—to come
back here and tell our enemies that they may take our
lives, but they'll never take . . . *our freedom!*[7]

If this were a movie (the latter scene is, of course), it's at this point
you should hear the soundtrack abruptly stop and the screen freeze.
Why? Because reality hits . . . and it's got a different version. A less
glamorized, less heroic one. I'm sure you know by now that our quest
for freedom doesn't instantly mean our situation will change. Your
struggle with pornography or anger or unbelief won't suddenly turn
a corner simply because you now have a new resolve to be free. No,
true liberty takes place first in the spirit, then *grows* into the natural.

FREEDOM BEGINS WITH FAITH BECAUSE IT IS A MATTER OF FAITH.

When Jesus healed
people, He routinely made
comments such as "Your
faith has made you well"
(e.g., Matthew 9:22; Mark
10:52; Luke 17:19). Freedom begins with faith because it *is* a matter
of faith. When we believe, abide in, and know the *logos* of God, revelation will eventually hit. And once that occurs, we'll find our spirit
changing the shape of our natural being. Faith will arise, and freedom—true, lasting freedom—will feel like it's just a breath away. It
may be mere moments away. Or it may come in a few more days or
months. Yet when we continue to stay in that place of seeing and recognizing truth by the spirit rather than by what appears in the natural, total freedom is inevitable.

Study any portion of the Bible and you'll notice that we always
receive from God *by faith* first. By its very definition, that means
believing in something we do not yet see (Hebrews 11:1). And that, of

course, goes against our *psuché* nature, which is governed by our own logic and reason. Living in a place of freedom requires this kingdom vision. It takes peering past the natural obstacles, overlooking your soulish condition, and knowing that, by faith, you are indeed free.

This is why I include "freedom" as a step in the process and then move on to "freedom indeed." Jesus did the same. He spoke of being free, then free indeed. I've known far too many believers who've walked through the soul's liberation process and ended up 80, 90, even 98 percent free—yet that remaining fraction came back to haunt them.

If we fail to carry the process of freedom all the way to its completion, sooner or later that remnant of a certain stronghold will grow back to its former size, sometimes even returning bigger, stronger, and more alluring. And, eventually, that can spell total destruction. How many of us can name men or women of God who've had this happen in their lives? It's not uncommon to find ministers of the gospel who have hidden unconquered sins for twenty or thirty years suddenly brought to ruin. Maybe they felt they'd honestly dealt with a certain issue, yet because the process wasn't completed, it rose up again.

Satan is persistent. He has his demons working overtime, finding every possible sliver of opportunity, even if it takes half a lifetime. He'll chip away and chip away, often using things that seem harmless around us. Then, one day, we'll wake up and realize we're battling an even more powerful stronghold than we faced decades ago.

Sometimes, however, it isn't the devil who causes our past issues to reemerge and be exposed. Sometimes it's God Himself.

A few years ago I sensed the Holy Spirit repeatedly drawing my mind to an area of my life I felt I'd already dealt with twenty years prior. I asked God what He was doing. "I've already been through that," I explained to Him (because, as everyone knows, God needs things explained to Him). "Remember, Lord? You broke those things off of my *psuché*. Your *logos* cast down those faulty paradigms. I walked through 2 Corinthians 10:4–5 to a tee."

At about the same time an intercessor in my congregation came to me with a list of weaknesses in my life she believed God had shown her. She was kind and not at all presumptive. In fact, she said she didn't see them in my life, just felt that God had spoken them to her. They were pride, presumption, and fear of failure. The last one was what had been coming to my mind as well, and which I felt I had previously overcome.

I told her the same thing I told God: "I don't think so."

"Well, just pray about it," she said.

The first thing I did was tell God there was no way I had any pride in my life. "See," He answered. Ouch. Strike one against *psuché*.

"Well, I'm not presumptuous," I said. "I'm very careful to only do what You lead me to do."

"I will show you," was all He said.

Then, over the next three to four months, two out-of-town speaking engagements turned out disastrous. "How did this happen?" I complained to the Lord. "Where was Your blessing?"

"I didn't send you to those places," He said to me. "So you were on your own. Now, stop taking meetings just because they sound good and your calendar is open. In the future, your schedule is going to become very demanding and you must be very careful to go only where I send you." Strike two.

But when the fear-of-failure thing came up, that's when I said, "No way, God. I've already dealt with that."

"You're right," He replied, "you did overcome that. But I didn't get it all. I dealt with it to the degree that I could back then. Most of the root was destroyed, but now I want to get the rest of it. You were free enough for what I'd called you to do at that point, but now I must go deeper. If I don't, because of the situations you will find yourself in and the favor I want to give you, fear of failure could destroy you. Or, in the very least, keep you from seeing My full destiny for you accomplished."

How do you argue with God when He says something like that? And yet I did.

I lost, of course. Strike three. And after being convinced that, yes, parts of this issue were still in me, I set out to take the

IT'S ONE THING TO BE FREE. IT'S ANOTHER TO BE FREE INDEED.

exact same steps I'd taken two decades before. I went straight to God's Word and found His truth about the situation. I spoke those words into every part of my being. I meditated on them. Like a cow chewing cud, I digested the *logos*, brought it back up again, digested it again, brought it back up again ... and kept doing this until I'd absorbed every bit of nutrition I could. I abided in the truth of God, allowing Him to take His Word and cut me open again with its double-edged precision. He divided me up and gouged out the *psuché* strongholds that were still in there. And do you know what? God did exactly what He said He'd do, finishing the job all the way this time.

And Then Some

It's one thing to be free. It's another to be free *indeed,* the last of our five steps. We started this book in John 8, and that's where we'll end it as well. Jesus' promise of freedom wasn't a flippant suggestion but a guarantee: "If the Son makes you free, you will be free indeed" (v. 36). We know that God's Word, by its very nature, will not return void. We also know that as the only sinless man who ever walked the earth, Jesus Christ was not a liar. Keeping those two truths in mind, we can be assured that freedom isn't far away.

As we discussed in chapter 1, the word for "indeed" is *ontôs*. It denotes complete reality. One hundred percent. There isn't a slight chance of error or a 5 percent margin for fiction—it's entirely real. In fact, it's as real as Jesus' resurrection (see Luke 24:34).

As the final step of the liberation process to becoming who we are, we must seal the deal. Yes, Christ has already set our spirit free. And, yes, as we work the process of freedom our soul receives revelation of the truth, and in the deepest parts of our "knower" we have faith that we are free. We are who He says we are. Our soul is becoming free of the strongholds that held it back for so long.

But the "indeed" part of the process, the *ontôs*, requires seeing something through to the very end. We cannot stop until we reach the hundredfold stage of fruit. That is free *indeed*. Jesus said in Mark 4:8, "Other seeds fell into the good soil, and as they grew up and increased, they yielded a crop and produced thirty, sixty, and a hundredfold." That's what we're after.

Once again, it's like a woman carrying a baby—three months, six months, nine months, baby. Though the seed has been planted and life has been conceived, the process must be lived out. The baby must be cared for, protected, and nourished by Mama's body. And though she or he can't be seen, there are unmistakable signs. We *know* there's a baby in the womb. And then, at the end of nine months—baby!

Now, if you think one day there was no baby and the next day there was—just like that, nice and easy—do yourself a favor and don't say that to Mama. She just might educate you on the finer points of carrying and birthing a baby. In reality, we all know that when the seed is planted, we're just beginning a long but rewarding process of life.

And so it is with the seed of God's Word. We must nurture and feed that which has been planted in us. As it grows we will become ever more convinced that there is life growing in us. *Revelation is occurring. The knowledge of the truth is coming.* At some point, we'll be as certain of complete freedom as we would be if the process were finished. Faith has come. *Freedom is inevitable for our soul.* Then the birth takes place. Adam's sin is reversed, *psuché* is at the cross and yoked again to God, the stone is rolled away and our spirit is free to soar. We are free *indeed.*

Don't give up on your quest for freedom. Just as surely as there is a God in heaven, you can have it. The Lord is committed to overthrowing exalted *psuché* in your life, demolishing every unwholesome stronghold in your subconscious, and making you once again a spirit-led person.

A great story has made the rounds about a scrawny, seemingly undernourished old man who entered a restaurant and asked who he needed to see to get a job at a nearby lumberjack camp. "You won't need to go far," the restaurant owner replied as he pointed to a nearby booth. "The supervisor is having lunch right over there."

The jobseeker approached the supervisor and announced, "I'm looking for a lumberjack job." The boss politely tried to talk him out of the idea. Surely this weak old man wouldn't be able to fell a tree, let alone keep up with the daily quotas. "Give me a few minutes of your time and I'll show you what I can do," suggested the man.

When the two arrived at a grove needing to be cleared, the slender, persistent old man picked up an ax and proceeded to chop down a huge tree in record time. "That's incredible," the boss said. "Where did you learn to fell trees like that?"

"Well," replied the old man, "you've heard of the Sahara Forest?"

Hesitantly the boss replied, "Don't you mean the Sahara Desert?"

The old man produced a smile and said, "Sure, that's what it's called now."[8]

You've heard of a *pneumatikos?* Yeah, it used to be called *psuchikos,* but a man showed up with a sword . . .

ENDNOTES

Chapter 1

1. Leonard Shapiro, "The Hit That Changed a Career," *Washington Post* (11/18/05).

2. James S. Hewett, ed., *Illustrations Unlimited* (Wheaton, IL: Tyndale, 1988), 456.

3. James Strong, *Strong's Exhaustive Concordance of the Bible* (Nashville: Thomas Nelson, 1995), 3689.

4. All scriptural emphasis has been added by the author.

5. Craig Brian Larson, ed., *Illustrations for Preaching and Teaching: From* LEADERSHIP JOURNAL (Grand Rapids: Baker, 1993), 280. Adapted.

Chapter 2

1. Strong, 5245; *hupernikas*, from 5228, 3528.

2. Glenn Van Ekeren, *Speaker's Sourcebook II* (New York: Prentice Hall, 1994), 193.

3. Bob Phillips, *The Star-Spangled Quote Book* (Eugene, OR: Harvest House, 1997), 145.

4. Cited by Walter B. Knight in *Knight's Master Book of New Illustrations* (Grand Rapids: Eerdmans, 1956), 30.

5. R. Kent Hughes, *1001 Great Stories and Quotes* (Wheaton, IL: Tyndale, 1998), 155.

Chapter 3

1. Strong, 1823. The word is *demuwth*; the root is *damah*, meaning "to compare" (1819).

2. Spiros Zodhiates, *Hebrew-Greek Key Word Study Bible, New American Standard Bible* (Chattanooga: AMG, 1977), 1851.

3. C. S. Lewis, *Mere Christianity* (San Francisco: HarperCollins, 2001).

4. This is a definition compiled from several different lexicons and dictionaries. The number in *Strong's Exhaustive Concordance of the Bible* is 225.

5. Larson, *Illustrations for Preaching and Teaching*, 27, from Maxie Dunnam, *Jesus' Claims—Our Promises.*

6. Dutch Sheets, *Intercessory Prayer* (Ventura, CA: Regal, 1996).

Chapter 4

1. Zodhiates, 1725.

2. Strong, 5449, 5453.

3. Andrew Peyton Thomas, *Wall Street Journal* (8/9/95).

4. Larson, *Illustrations for Preaching and Teaching*, 167.

5. Strong, 3472.

6. Ibid., 2572.

7. Hughes, 10.

8. Strong, 5187.

Chapter 5

1. Daniel J. Boorstin, *The Discoverers* (New York: Vintage, 1993), 482.

2. *Merriam-Webster's Collegiate Dictionary*, 11th ed. (Springfield, MA: Merriam-Webster, Inc., 2003), 1241.

3. Hans Moravec, "When Will Computer Hardware Match the Human Brain?" *Journal of Evolution and Technology*, Vol. 1 (2: 1998).

4. Ibid., 8.

5. Arthur Conan Doyle, *A Study in Scarlet* (Philadelphia: J. B. Lippincott, 1890), 12.

6. Strong, 3794.

7. Ibid., 2192.

8. Norman Vincent Peale, *Power of the Plus Factor* (Old Tappan, NJ: Revell, 1987), adapted.

9. Details changed to protect those involved.

10. George Sweeting, *Great Quotes and Illustrations* (Waco: Word, 1985), 247.

11. Strong, 8176.

12. *Reader's Digest* (January 1996), 50.

13. Linda-Ann Stewart, "Myth Conceptions About Hypnosis," *Cedar-fire* (5/5/99), *www.cedarfire.com.*

Chapter 6

1. Strong, 4487.

2. Walter B. Knight, *Knight's Treasury of Illustrations* (Grand Rapids: Eerdmans, 1963), 181.

3. Jack Canfield and Mark Victor Hansen, *Chicken Soup for the Soul* (Deerfield Beach, FL: Health Communications, Inc., 1993), 290. Adapted.

4. Strong, 1834.

5. From Knight, *Knight's Treasury of Illustrations.* Adapted.

6. Hughes, 344–45.

Chapter 7

1. Strong, 313.

2. Zodhiates, 1882.

3. Strong, 4701.

4. Ibid., 4309.

5. Ibid., 4286.

6. From *www.wikipedia.org.*

7. Adapted from Sally Jenkins, "Biff, Crash, Bang: Jacobellis Loses Chance to Show Off a Gold Medal," *Washington Post* (2/18/06), E01.

8. Strong, 3339.

9. Ibid., 4964.

10. Ibid., 1381.

11. Craig Brian Larson, *Choice Contemporary Stories and Illustrations for Preachers, Teachers, and Writers* (Grand Rapids: Baker, 1998), 66.

Chapter 8

1. Strong, 4625.

2. Zodhiates, 1809.

3. Strong, 3341.

4. Edward K. Rowell, ed., *Fresh Illustrations for Preaching and Teaching: From* LEADERSHIP JOURNAL (Grand Rapids: Christianity Today and Baker, 1997), 26. Adapted.

Chapter 9

1. David Williams, "Fined for Being 'In Two Different Places at the Same Time,'" *Evening Standard* (5/25/05).

2. Craig Brian Larson, *Contemporary Illustrations* (Grand Rapids: Baker, 1996), 119–20.

3. A. W. Tozer, *The Root of the Righteous* (Camp Hill, PA: Christian Publications, 1986), 156.

Chapter 10

1. Zodhiates, 1887.

2. Larson, *Illustrations for Preaching and Teaching*, 134.

3. Zodhiates, 1773.

4. Ibid., 1718.

5. Strong, 1580.

6. Larson, 93.

7. Zodhiates, 1782.

8. *www.forgivenforlife.com/1a-testimony.html.*

Chapter 11

1. Thomas à Kempis, *The Imitation of Christ* (Milwaukee: Bruce, 1949), 11.

2. Strong, 1869.

3. Zodhiates, 1733.

4. Strong, 1949.

5. Dietrich Bonhoeffer, *The Cost of Discipleship* (New York: SCM, 1959).

Chapter 12

1. Dana Blanton, "More Believe in God Than Heaven," FOXNews (6/18/04), foxnews.com.

2. *Newsweek*/Beliefnet national poll of 1,004 adults (beliefnet.com), as reported by Jerry Adler, "In Search of the Spiritual," *Newsweek* (8/29/05), 46.

3. Josh McDowell and Bob Hostetler, *The New Tolerance* (Wheaton, IL: Tyndale, 1998), 174.

4. "Americans Donate Billions to Charity, But Giving to Churches Has Declined," The Barna Group (4/25/05), Barna.org.

5. Walter A. Elwell, ed. *The Shaw Pocket Bible Handbook* (Wheaton, IL: Harold Shaw, 1984), 348–49.

6. Zodhiates, 1853.

7. Source unknown.

8. Strong, 3307.

9. Zodhiates, 1855.

10. David A. Seamands, *Healing for Damaged Emotions* (Wheaton, IL: Victor, 1986), 61.

11. Jack Eicholz, *Homemade* (December 1989).

12. Seamands, 59.

13. Zodhiates, 1832.

14. Ibid., 1816.

15. Ibid., 1839.

Chapter 13

1. Larson, *Choice Contemporary Stories*, 88. Adapted.

2. Larson, *Contemporary Illustrations*, 281.

3. Strong, 1338.

4. Seamands, 23.

5. Strong, 3311.

6. Ibid., 5136.

7. Adapted from *Our Daily Bread* devotional entry, *www.elbourne.org/sermons/*.

8. *www.wikipedia.com*.

9. Zodhiates, 1846.

10. Ibid., 1861.

11. Strong, 1897.

12. Zodhiates, 1861.

Chapter 14

1. Zodhiates, 1763.

2. James Dobson, *Life on the Edge* (Dallas: Word, 1995), 134.

3. Larson, *Choice Contemporary Stories*, 239. Adapted.

4. Strong, 4920.

5. Warren Wiersbe, *Listening to the Giants* (Grand Rapids: Baker, 1980), 198.

Chapter 15

1. Joshua Benton, "Analysis Suggests Cheating on TAKS," *Dallas Morning News* (5/23/06).

2. Strong, 1097.

3. From *www.wikipedia.org*.

4. Strong, 225.

5. From Abraham Lincoln's speech on September 11, 1858. John Bartlett, *Bartlett's Familiar Quotations* (Boston: Little, Brown, and Company, 1863, 1980), 521.

6. From Abraham Lincoln's reply on February 23, 1861. Peter

Marshall and David Manuel, *The Glory of America* (Bloomington, MN: Garborg's, 1991), 2.23.

7. *Braveheart,* Paramount Pictures (1995).

8. Glenn Van Ekeren, *Speaker's Sourcebook II* (New York: Prentice Hall, 1994), 10.

Pray With Power and Purpose

At the heart of all conflict on earth is the question "Who is in charge?" In this powerful book, bestselling author Dutch Sheets reminds believers that God is in charge and He intends His people to be overcomers. Sheets paints a clear picture of the power God has reserved for His children to advance His Kingdom. Christians don't need to allow sin, Satan, or the circumstances of life to keep them from God's amazing promises. *Authority in Prayer* shows readers how to take hold of God's promises and change their world through prayer. This book is for all believers who want to live in greater freedom and godly authority, starting with powerful, effective prayer lives.